REVELATION for TODAY

REVELATION *for* TODAY

An Apocalyptic Approach

James M. Efird

Abingdon Press

Nashville

Revelation for Today: An Apocalyptic Approach

Copyright © 1989 by Abingdon Press

This book is printed on acid-free paper.

Library of Congress Cataloging-in-Publication Data

Efird, James M.
   Revelation for today : an apocalyptic approach / James M.
Efird.
     p.   cm.
   Bibliography: p.
   ISBN 0-687-36172-9 (pbk. : alk. paper)
   1. Bible. N.T. Revelation—Criticism, interpretation, etc.
2. Apocalyptic literature. I. Title
BS2825.2.E36   1989
228'.07—dc19   88-22187
                                                            CIP
ISBN-13: 978-0-687-36172-4

07 —17 16 15

MANUFACTURED IN THE UNITED STATES OF AMERICA

For my wife,
Vivian,
who has brought real beauty
into my life

CONTENTS

REVELATION *for* TODAY

PREFACE

Of all the biblical writings, the book of Revelation is the most feared, misunderstood, misused, and abused. There are reasons for this, some historical and some psychological, but in all the confusion many people despair of being able to interpret the book properly or of ever making any sense of it. The truth is, however, that Revelation is not that difficult to understand, if one realizes that this book represents a particular literary genre, which was developed in late postexilic Judaism to serve as a vehicle to carry messages of hope to people under persecution or extreme duress. The literary style is known by the term *apocalyptic*.

Literature written in this style flourished from about 200 B.C. to A.D. 100 and was characterized by rather wild and weird images and exaggerated symbols. These images and symbols, while meaningless to us in our culture, would have been quite understandable to those for whom the books were written. Typically in such works, if there was the possibility of any confusion, the author would explain the scene for the readers or hearers. If the people then could understand the writings, people today can as well if they learn about that literary style. Perhaps the closest analogy for modern times is our use of the political cartoon. That genre uses caricature, exaggerated symbols, and the imagina-

11

tion to get across the point of view of the cartoonist. Similarly the apocalyptic writers used the same methods in a literary style to get across their message.

Again, that literary genre was part of the culture of those times; it *would* have been quite understandable to the people for whom these books were written. People today understand political cartoons without a great amount of interpretation. For example, if several years ago, someone had seen a political cartoon that depicted a huge bear with missiles for teeth, crushing in its paw an airliner with people falling out into the water below while others peered out of the window with terror-stricken faces, and across the tail of the plane was painted KAL 007, no one would have had to have the meaning of that scenario explained. Anyone who was a part of our culture and who knew anything about what was going on in the world would understand exactly what all these symbols meant. So too with people in those biblical times when apocalyptic symbolism and imagery were common.

For persons today to understand books like Revelation written from the apocalyptic perspective, the history and background of that book must be understood as fully as possible. The book must then be read from the perspective of those people for whom it was originally intended and of the author who wrote it. If that can be done, the mystery will be solved and the meaning of the book will become clear. Revelation is not really all that difficult to understand if the interpreter will view it *consistently* as an apocalyptic work. That will be the approach in this examination of Revelation.

My present book is not intended for experts in the field of apocalyptic study. It is intended for pastors and laypersons in the church to assist them in learning how to interpret apocalyptic literature correctly, specifically the book of Revelation. That book has for too long been left to those who do not really understand it and who have made of it something that it was never intended to be, namely, a time table for "the end." Revelation is a classic example of apocalyptic literature, and this exposition is designed to introduce people to the proper understanding of and approach to this type of writing. Such a study can be and is exciting and beneficial, both intellectually and spiritually.

Words of appreciation are due to so many for help in my own pilgrimage to the understanding of Revelation and in the writing of this book. To all my former teachers, especially Julian Price Love of Louisville Presbyterian Theological Seminary, I owe a great debt in learning how to approach the Bible so as to understand it properly. To my students both in the Duke Divinity School and in many classes in churches who have challenged, questioned, and encouraged me in my attempt to understand and present Revelation properly and fairly, a hearty note of appreciation is directed. There was one old gentleman in a church in Tennessee whose words have remained with me in this endeavor. After hearing Revelation presented as an apocalyptic work, he said, "Why haven't we been told this before? We have needed to hear this!"

Finally, a word of appreciation is always owed to the members of one's family who tolerate the author's moods, deadlines, and work schedule. To them I owe more than I can repay, especially my wife, Vivian, who has typed this manuscript (twice) and who has supported me in so many ways.

James M. Efird

INTRODUCTION

The Development of Apocalyptic Thought and Literature

The most important consideration for properly understanding the mysterious and wondrous book of Revelation lies in the interpreter's understanding of and becoming comfortable with a movement that developed and blossomed in later postexilic Judaism (after 538 B.C.). This phenomenon is known as the "Apocalyptic" movement. In order to make some sense of the strange and weird images and symbols found in Revelation (compare also Daniel 7–12 and many apocalyptic works which were not included in the canon of the Scripture) one must become aware of where and how the basic apocalyptic thought-pattern originated and how that thought-pattern was finally placed into a literary genre (or type) to serve as a vehicle for transmitting the basic message of this ideology.

It is not the purpose of this study to go into meticulous detail with regard to the various technical theories about the origins of the apocalyptic movement. Some scholars argue that it developed from the prophetic movement of Old Testament times; others that it was rooted in the Wisdom movement; still others emphasize the sociological origins of the phenomenon; yet another idea anchors the movement in Persian thought. There is probably some truth in each of these claims since portions of each can be clearly detected in the apocalyptic thought-pattern and literature. The method used here will be that of attempting to show how these different elements were in fact blended together to form apocalyptic thought and literature in Judaism and, later, Christianity.

Historical Setting

The Judean kingdom was destroyed by the Babylonians in 586 B.C. Jerusalem was sacked and burned, as was the Temple, and the countryside likewise was laid waste. Most of the people were taken into Babylonia as captives and exiles. It was at this time that the prophets, who had previously predicted the destruction of the land and nation, began to talk about a return to the homeland, the re-establishment of the community in Judea once more. Jeremiah, Ezekiel, and the great prophet of Isaiah 40–55 all looked forward to the return. Interestingly enough they were not as clear in their thinking about the precise nature and shape of the new community as they were in their conviction that these people would be allowed to return.

Jeremiah, for example, talked about a new "Branch" (meaning a ruler from the Davidic line, Jeremiah 23:5-6), but he also talked of a new community, which would be governed by a "new covenant" established directly between God and the people (cf. Jeremiah 31). The specific "form" of this restored group is not, therefore, precisely described.

Ezekiel also spoke of a Davidic "prince" (cf. Ezek. 34:24), but he then described the restored community as a theocratic state governed by priests centered in a new Temple in Jerusalem (cf. Ezekiel 40–48).

In the prophets of the early period after the return (ca. 538–450 B.C.) there seems to have been similar confusion about whether the new state would be one governed by a Davidic king (cf. Hag. 2:20-23) or whether the community would have a priest as leader (cf. Zech. 6:9-14). The truth was that even though the Persians, who defeated the Babylonians in 539 B.C. and became the dominant power over this part of the world for more than 200 years, allowed the Judean people to return (not all did, however), they were not about to allow these people to establish an independent political state. Judea was to be a part of the fairly sophisticated provincial administration the Persian government had established for the oversight of its huge empire.

After the initial burst of enthusiasm and unfounded optimism had begun to fade, the Jewish people in Palestine settled down to attempt to make a life for themselves in this setting. It was extremely difficult, however, for they were economically impoverished, politically powerless, and militarily defenseless. The land lay in ruins. Everything had to be rebuilt from practically nothing. The Temple was finally rebuilt in 520–515 B.C., but Jerusalem had not yet been rebuilt or inhabited. That process did not come about until 444 and 432 B.C. with the ministry of Nehemiah, a Jewish servant from the court of the Persian king. His work among the people in Judea coupled with the ministry of Ezra, a scribe from Babylonia, set the agenda for Judaism for some time to come. The community became basically a theocracy, at least internally, and the Temple and priesthood served as the focus for Jewish life in Palestine. One addition to this scenario came around 400–350 B.C. when the *Torah* was accepted as "canonical," that is, it was understood to be authoritative for the life, faith, and practice of the community in Judea, and later for all Jews.

The historical and social circumstances did not improve appreciably with the passage of time. Even though the people tried to be faithful servants of God, everything seemed to be against them. Years, even centuries, began to roll by—and still no improvement, still no independent political existence. This set of circumstances caused something of a religious or theological crisis. The prevailing "theology" of the Jewish community at this time is described as "Deuteronomic theology," named for the dominant ideology of the "Deuteronomic History" (i.e., Deuteronomy, [Joshua], Judges, Samuel, and Kings). With regard to one's fortune in the world, this ideology taught that if one would keep God's laws, one would be rewarded with a good life, health, success, and happiness. If one disobeyed God's laws, evil would surely dominate the life of the person or the community. Therefore, if people were suffering, that situation was surely the result of sin and rebellion against God.

The basic theology of the prophets was Deuteronomic. The people had sinned; the nations (Israel and Judah) had been destroyed. Now, however, the judgment was past; the people had returned after the judgment and were attempting to keep the laws of God as best they could; but the suffering continued. The old theology no longer "fit" the current experiences of the community. What was wrong? The question was pressing: "Why are we still suffering and suffering so intensely?" An answer was needed.

Introduction

In this setting two religious movements began to emerge in the Jewish community. The Wisdom movement, which had its roots in Israel's past, began to blossom more fully. Every Wisdom movement has two basic components, one practical and the other more speculative. From this latter dimension came wrestlings with the question, Why? "Why are we suffering when we do not deserve it?" The books of Job and Ecclesiastes in particular attempted to wrestle with the problem. Even though the answers these two books propose are fascinating and insightful, it is not the purpose of this study to dwell on them (for a discussion of these ideas, cf. James M. Efird, *Biblical Books of Wisdom*, Valley Forge, Pa.: Judson Press, 1983).

The emphasis in this study is on the second of these movements, namely, the apocalyptic. When the people of Judah exiled in Babylonia returned to their homeland in 538 B.C., the Persian Empire had just begun to spread its influence over this part of the ancient world. For more than two hundred years the peoples of Palestine, Egypt, Asia Minor, old Assyria, and Babylonia, along with the Persian homeland itself (present-day Iran), were under the domination of Persian rule. In addition to political control and influence, Persian ideas began to influence the thinking of these subject people. (One would be most surprised if that had not been true.) Such was the case with the Hebrew people as well.

Persian religious thought (stated in brief) held that there were two coeternal powers or forces in the universe, one good and one evil, which were locked in a life-and-death struggle for superiority over the created order. All of the cosmos was involved in this conflict, and all parts of creation were called upon to choose which side they were on. There was no middle ground. The earth and its people as a part of the

19

created universe had to choose where their allegiance would lie—with good or evil. The conflict would continue until the *end,* when there would come a final cataclysmic battle. The powers and forces of good would be victorious; the world as we know it would be destroyed; and those who had allied themselves with good would reap their reward (as would those who had allied themselves with evil).

This dualism, cosmic spiritual good vs. cosmic spiritual evil, gradually became a part of the thought-patterns of the Hebrew people. It is not really difficult to understand the reason. Here was a people suffering intensely in spite of all their efforts to keep God's laws and to live as they believed God wanted them to live. According to the Deuteronomic theology they should be prospering not destitute, victorious not defeated. The Persian ideology gave them an alternative interpretation for their situation. After all, in the continuing conflict between good and evil (in which our world participates), there are three possible scenarios that may come about. First, there are those periods when good has the upper hand over evil. In such a time good people would be protected and prosper; in short, the Deuteronomic theology would certainly "fit" this setting. Second, there are those periods when good and evil are at a stalemate, that is, neither has the upper hand. Again in such a period good people would normally be rewarded and evil people would usually receive their just deserts. Deuteronomic theology again would seem to be "true" in such a setting.

In this continuing struggle, however, there do come those times when evil gains control and dominates a segment of history. On these occasions those who are allied with good will suffer and be persecuted, and here the Deuteronomic theology will not fit. The answer to the problem of why good people are suffering would not then be explained by resorting to a theory that they have done evil, but rather the answer is that the good people are persecuted in this setting *because* they are good, *because* they remain faithful and loyal even and especially in times of hostility and domination by the powers of evil. Such thinking certainly appealed, obviously, to the Jewish community suffering in Palestine They knew they were trying to keep God's laws; they knew they were experiencing harsh times and persecution at the hands of others around them. How could this be explained? Certainly the Deuteronomic ideology could not be used to make sense of such terrible times. One could understand and accept this situation, however, if one believed that the suffering and evil times were the result of one of those moments in the great cosmic struggle where evil has control. In such times those who have chosen to stand on the side of good *will* suffer—not because they are evil and deserve to suffer but because they are fighting on the side of right. It is not difficult to understand why this thought-pattern became a part of the Jewish mind-set in postexilic times.

One must not, however, think that the Hebrew people simply accepted these ideas without altering them. The Hebrews did borrow some ideas as they progressed through their history and were influenced by the movements of history, but they always made whatever they borrowed conform to their basic understandings of the revelation of their God. For example, they could not accept the idea of a power or force of evil coexisting with God from the beginning. They could, however, accept the dualism that they saw in the world between good and evil. They could also understand and explain their suffering in the light of these new insights.

For example, the Hebrew people did not really think of "eternity" in the same way as the later Greeks or modern philosophers and theologians. Hebrew thought held basically that God had created the world and worked in and through the continuing process of history to relate to that creation. There was no real idea of an "end" of history or the created order, at least during the period when the books of the Hebrew canon were composed (to ca. 165 B.C.). There are numerous places in the English translations of the Hebrew Scriptures, unfortunately, where one encounters the terms *forever, everlasting*, and similar phrasing. The truth is that these readings of the Hebrew terms are very misleading, since the proper understanding of these words and phrases should be "for a long time," or "for a certain designated period of time." For example, in Job 7:16, Job is bewailing his terrible condition and situation, and many English texts translate part of this passage "I would not live forever." Actually Job has no concept of living "forever" in the modern sense; what is intended in the text is for Job to state that he does not wish to live out his "allotted" days, that is, his designated period of time.

This insight should alert the interpreter of the Hebrew Scriptures to a proper understanding of the thought-patterns of the Jewish people, and one also then can understand more clearly why the Hebrews had some difficulty dealing with ideas about *the end* in the Persian sense. Therefore Persian thought when brought over into the Jewish setting was altered to describe a concept of two ages. Rather than concentrate on *the end* at the close of history, the Jewish apocalyptists tended to focus on a two-age motif, a present age of suffering, and a new age or era with persecution removed. The present evil age was ruled by the demonic powers and forces of evil (which usually did their evil work through human agents, however). After evil had run its course (in fact, God "allowed" this to take place), God or God's agent would intervene, destroy the evil persecutor, and establish a new age with the persecution eliminated. This new age was not in heaven nor did it come with the end of history as we know it; rather the new age was a continuation of history. And later, as history progressed, the powers and forces of evil might once again gain control. In such a time evil would prosper, the righteous people of God suffer and be persecuted, and another apocalyptic era would have emerged. This was the basic message of Jewish apocalyptic. In some later apocalyptic works, once Greek influence also began to be exerted on Hebrew thought, there were some writings that did concentrate on *the end*. Which of these two ideas is presented in any apocalyptic work, however, will have to be determined by the text of the book itself, not on an *a priori* presupposition that any apocalyptic writer always talks about *the end*. That is simply not the case.

Most Hebrew (and later Christian) apocalyptic writings emerge from a period of persecution or difficult times. The thought-pattern became clearly defined; what was needed was a literary form to serve as a vehicle to carry the message to the people. One, in fact, was devised. The literary form that emerged to serve as a vehicle for the presentation of apocalyptic thought developed into a highly symbolic literature, full of weird and even bizarre figures and images. These symbols seem to be remarkably consistent in their basic connotations, differing only as the historical circumstances and settings change from time to time and place to place.

Perhaps the most important and fundamental

component of an apocalyptic work is the vision. Every apocalyptic writing consists of a series of visions, usually self-contained and not necessarily arranged with any concrete pattern or chronology in mind. About the most that can be said is that the apocalyptic "seer" begins by assuming that a persecution is in progress and concludes with a symbolic description of the end of that persecution and a description of a new age with the persecution removed. The content or "revelation" (*apocalypse* means "revelation" in Greek) of these visions is presented in highly symbolic images the "seer" does not understand. There is then an interpreter present who explains the meaning of the scene, usually in very straightforward terms. The older idea that apocalyptic was written in a code so that the persecutors could not understand and thus further intimidate the persecuted people simply does not hold up under close examination. If the persecutors could read the symbolic vision, they could certainly read the explanation!

In the visionary scenes several standard components almost always appear. First, there are beasts with heads and horns, grotesque and hideous in appearance. The beasts always represent nations, and the heads and horns usually represent rulers (kings, emperors). What nation is being described always depends on the historical situation the apocalyptic writer is addressing. In fact many of these visions are "historical surveys" describing symbolically how the course of history had brought the persecuted people to that point in time, and usually there was included a symbolic description of the future (the immediate future) depicting the new age, which was about to arrive with the persecutor having been removed from the scene.

Additional symbols include numbers and colors, each of which has a designated import. The numbers that are significant in apocalyptic are 3, 4, 7, 10, 12, and 3 1/2. It is very important to apply with consistency the meaning of the number (or its multiple) when interpreting apocalyptic works. Three designates the realm of the spirit; four denotes that which is related to the created order. Seven suggests completeness in the sense of that which has come to maturity or appropriate fulfillment. Ten is similar to seven, but ten usually suggests the idea of completeness with the nuance of inclusiveness. Twelve signifies the people of God, and three and one half is always used to symbolize the length of time that evil is allowed to run its course, persecuting the people of God. Sometimes the numbers are combined in such a way as to symbolize a larger point the author wishes to make. For example, the mysterious number in Revelation of which so much has been made—144,000—is a combination of a multiple of ten and a multiple of twelve, thus signifying the full or total number of the people of God.

Colors are also significant. White is the most commonly found color in apocalyptic literature and symbolizes victory. The martyrs are always given white robes, which denote their ultimate victory over the powers and forces of evil. Red often occurs, indicating war or conflict. Black denotes the lack of something, the lack of food in famine, or the lack of health in pestilence or plague. In Revelation there is another color, greenish-gray (the RSV translates this color "pale"), which is the color of a corpse and thus represents death.

All of these "standard" symbolic images are combined in every individual apocalyptic work to depict in a somewhat bizarre way certain ideas that

Revelation for Today

would be meaningful and beneficial to the people for whom the book was originally intended. These visionary scenes are overwhelming in their magnitude and breadth. One of the problems in the attempt to interpret an apocalyptic work correctly lies in the area of how far does one go in attributing specific symbolism to the images in the visions. Some interpreters want to find meaning in every detail of the vision, but this seems to be going much too far, making the visionary scene into some sort of tightly knit allegory. As in the modern political cartoon, one can certainly ascertain the thrust of the caricature without finding hidden meaning under every detail in the drawing. One must exercise some degree of common sense in attempting to determine what is intended by the author to be understood as specific symbolism and what is "window dressing" to enhance the overall impact of the message. Such distinctions require deliberate sensitivity to the intention of the original author and the original audience being addressed. Perhaps no two persons will ever agree fully on the interpretation of all the symbolic details found in Revelation, but the overall message of the author will not be difficult to discover if one is sensitive to the historical setting and the overall message of the book as an apocalyptic work. Again one is reminded that in most apocalyptic works what the author wishes the reader to understand clearly is explained, usually in precise and specific terms.

To be sure, in apocalyptic literature the imagery and symbolism are painted in large, even grotesque figures. The images were overdrawn and grotesque, however, because the situations addressed by these writings were greatly significant not only for the people who were caught up in a persecution or evil

26

times, but because the issues involved extended far beyond this world. What was being experienced and participated in by the people of God was part of the cosmic struggle between good and evil. The sacrifices made and the victories won were to be part of that final conquest of evil by good, wherever and whenever that moment would come. What was important for them was the *present* struggle and the call for endurance *now*. To read each apocalyptic work as if it were foretelling the end of the world, therefore, is to read into the text a meaning before determining what the book actually intended to teach. Thus in interpreting apocalyptic one must be sensitive to what apocalyptic literature is and what the original setting of the particular book under consideration was. It is always a call for faithfulness in the midst of persecution for the causes of God in evil times.

The History of the Interpretation of Revelation

As already noted apocalyptic literature flourished between 200 B.C. and A.D. 100. Partly because the Christians were so heavily influenced by apocalyptic thought and partly because the Jewish community itself was becoming more Hellenized (i.e., more influenced by Greek thought and ideas) and was being pushed away from its Palestinian roots, the apocalyptic movement basically ceased to be a factor in the development of Judaism after about A.D. 100. Of all the apocalyptic books produced by this community, only one made its way into the final collection of the Hebrew canon—the book of Daniel. It is interesting that Daniel is only half apocalyptic. Chapters 7–12 contain a series of apocalyptic visions, but chapters 1–6 contain a series of popular wisdom stories. Daniel was included in the canon (humanly speaking) because it served as the basis for the feast of Hanukkah, which commemorated the lifting of the proscription against Judaism by the Seleucid King Antiochus IV in 167–164 B.C.

The early Christians were very much into apocalyptic ideology, and that thinking was very much a part of the Christian mind-set. By about A.D. 100, however, the church had been cut off from its Palestinian origins and had, in fact, become basically a Gentile movement. Though the church accepted and embraced its origins in Judaism, the members of the church did not really understand fully the teachings of the Hebrew Scriptures in general and apocalyptic thinking in particular. Since the apocalyptic literature and mind-set was so firmly grounded in Palestinian Judaism, and since the church was now cut off from this heritage, and since the Jewish community itself had eschewed apocalyptic, the key to properly understanding this literature began rapidly to be lost. By the middle to the end of the second century A.D., the church fathers were extremely puzzled about the book. Partly because of uncertainty in interpreting the book and partly because many (even then) were using the book to espouse all sorts of wild schemes and scenarios many Christian leaders did not think that Revelation should be accepted as a part of the Christian canon—a view still held by some! The debate continued literally for centuries until the end of the fourth century A.D. when the church's leadership agreed basically on the twenty-seven documents that now constitute the New Testament. Revelation was included in this collection. Thus the church and its constituency had to deal with the problem of how to interpret this strange and bizarre book, which seemed even more strange and bizarre as the years rolled along.

Space does not permit a detailed history of the interpretation of the book of Revelation through the centuries of the church's history, but there are several main ideas that seem to be consistent problems. One problem stems from the approach to the various "episodes" in the book: Are these to be understood literally or symbolically; are they descriptions of what happened or what is to happen; are they to be interpreted as presenting a historical progression of events or only several descriptions of the same event or events? Each of these questions had been debated by various interpreters through the years, and the strengths and weaknesses of each position will be discussed later in the exposition of the text.

There are really three areas of interpretation that are extremely important to the proper understanding of Revelation and which are at the heart of a legitimate interpretation of the text. These three are (1) the numbered cycles of 7 (the seven seals, 6:1–8:1; the seven trumpets, 8:1–11:19; and the seven bowls of the wrath of God, 15–16); (2) the two historical surveys (chs. 12–14 and 17–19); and (3) the thousand-year reign of Jesus with the saints (20:4-7), usually known as the millennium. All of these components of Revelation have been discussed and have been controversial over the years, but the millennium has been the most heavily debated. What this thousand-year period means in the context of the book itself will be clarified in the exposition of the text, but a history of the church's wrestling with understanding Revelation can be illustrated by concentrating on this aspect alone.

In the second century many groups within Christendom naturally attempted to understand the book of Revelation. For the most part these people still held to a return of Jesus very soon (as the early church certainly believed), and several believed that the millennium, an earthly kingdom, would begin after Jesus returned. Such a belief later came to be known as premillennial, that is, that Jesus would return before the thousand-year reign. Justin Martyr and Irenaeus, second-century leaders, both believed in a worldly kingdom that would be established after Jesus returned.

As time passed and Jesus did not return, however, many interpreters began to suggest other ideas. Although in this early period many still looked forward to the establishment of the millennium, some began to argue for certain dates in the future when the thousand years would begin. Hippolytus in the early third century believed that the millennium would begin in A.D. 500. Because of certain groups, however, especially the Montanists, who were espousing elaborate schemes involving the thousand-year period, there emerged a "spiritualizing" or symbolic interpretation of the book. Interestingly enough, some accepted a symbolic interpretation of Revelation overall but still held to a literal understanding of the thousand years. In short, during the first four centuries of Christian interpretation, Revelation was (as were some other New Testament books) understood partly symbolically, partly literally; the details varied from person to person and place to place. One significant change came at the point of the millennium—some began to see this period as the church in the world presently until the return of Jesus at the end. This was the beginning of the interpretative idea called postmillennialism, that is, that Jesus would return after the thousand years.

By the fifth century the approach to Revelation was primarily one of viewing this book as thoroughly "spiritualistic"; that is, all of the book was to be understood as symbolic. The millennium continued to be understood in both symbolic and literal ways, however. Most believed that the church in the world was the thousand-year reign, however that might be defined and whatever the purpose might be. Whether the thousand years were to be understood literally or symbolically was still hotly debated. About the year 1000, people began to grow nervous, thinking that the end was very near. When 1000 came and went, as did 1100 and then 1200, most settled down into a completely symbolic understanding of this time reference. They believed that Christ was reigning in the church in the world and would do so until the time came for Jesus' return and the finalizing of all things. The millennium was "in process."

With the Protestant Reformation some of the approaches to Revelation began to be altered. Since the reformers identified the Roman Catholic Church as the beast (cf. chs. 13 and 17) and the wounded head (ch. 13) and the harlot (ch. 17) as the Pope, a new emphasis, led by Roman Catholic interpreters, emerged. This emphasis pointed in the direction of what the book meant to its own time and place, an emphasis on the book in its original historical setting and meaning. During this period, from the Reformation to the present time, all the different approaches have been used, some interpreting the book symbolically, some literally, but perhaps most combining the two in various ways.

As is obvious the church was continuing the struggle to interpret Revelation properly, but the task was frustrating. No "key" was yet available to give some insight into the theological and literary phenomenon of "apocalyptic." It was not until the rise and development of critical investigation and historical research in the late eighteenth and early nineteenth centuries that the slow process of discovering other apocalyptic works from the 200 B.C. to A.D. 100 time frame and analyzing these documents that scholars finally began to understand how apocalyptic thought and literature operated. From the study of this large number of apocalyptic books, the thought, message, symbolism, method, and so forth of this literary style have begun to be clearer as more research and study have been undertaken. Even with all this additional knowledge at our disposal, the church, unfortunately, has made very little progress toward a proper understanding of how to approach and interpret Revelation.

It will be the goal of this exposition of Revelation to apply the apocalyptic method of interpretation to this apocalyptic book as consistently as possible. If the reader can learn to think apocalyptically and to read the book (or listen to it read) as one of those for whom it was originally written, the chances are very high that Revelation can be understood properly. Once the original meaning can be determined, one can then seek to apply the teachings and principles of the document to modern times.

Excursus

Many people today have been exposed to a particular form of interpretation of the book of Revelation that is part of a larger theological system. This system is variously known by such terms as

Introduction

Bible prophecy, premillennial end-times, or by its more precise title, *dispensationalism.* This system and its many different "varieties" are widely known primarily through radio and television preachers and through many popular books written from that perspective. The influence of this system has been very permeative in Christian circles affecting the teaching of many who do not accept the entire philosophy but who have accepted parts of that system into their own.

Contrary to popular belief this ideology and interpretative method have not been in existence for the entire history of the church. They have been developed over only the past 160 years, having first been espoused in their present form in the first half of the nineteenth century. In the early part of that century, there was a great deal of dissatisfaction with the established church in Great Britain and Ireland. Many persons formed small "cell" groups, apart from the formal ecclesiastical structures and rituals, for the basic purpose of Bible study, prayer, and fellowship. The leaders of this movement finally severed ties with the established church and these groups coalesced together to form the movement known as the Plymouth Brethren. Their idea was that the established church was rotten and corrupt and that there was really only a small remnant left in the church who were faithful, loyal, and "true-blue" believers.

Joining himself with this group of people was an Irish Anglican priest named John Nelson Darby. This man was committed to understanding the Bible and zealous in his pursuit of a particular type of biblical interpretation. He became one of the most articulate and "high-profile" leaders of the Plymouth Brethren movement. Studying the Bible intently during a period of convalescence for an injured leg (1827–1829), Darby came to certain conclusions. He believed that the entire history of God's dealing with the world was included in the Bible from creation to the *end*. He further believed that God dealt with the world through the nation of Israel. Since the Jewish community had rejected Jesus as Messiah when he came, God created the church to serve as a type of "interim institution" until God would be able to complete God's work in the world through the nation of Israel. The church was really an "afterthought" or a "parenthesis," as Darby liked to call it.

The church must be removed, therefore, when the final moments and events begin to unfold. How could that be since the church had served as a useful component in God's plan? First of all, the church would decline, and the abuses of the church seen in Darby's time were proof enough that there were really very few true believers left. Thus there were only a small number with whom to deal, but what about those people? Darby and his followers used a passage from Paul to explain this problem. In I Thessalonians 4:13-18, Paul uses symbolic language to explain to the people of Thessalonica that they and their loved ones would ultimately be reunited in God's kingdom. Darby, however, understood this passage to be the means whereby the church would be removed from the world before the final scene of God's dealing with the world would begin. This idea has come to be known as the Rapture—the catching up out of this world the faithful of the church. Other passages were called in to support this theory, but none of them really has anything to teach about a "rapture." (For a fuller discussion of this and other aspects of the Darbyists' system, see James M. Efird,

Introduction

End-Times: Rapture, Antichrist, Millennium, Nashville: Abingdon Press, 1986.)

The followers of Darby then began to search the biblical texts in such a way as to add supporting "evidence" and additional scenarios to the events connected with the *end*. Naturally the apocalyptic literature in the Bible became a focal point for their investigation, and these books were read without any consideration of what they meant in their original time and place but only as predictions of the events that would accompany the final end-times scene. The beast of Revelation 13 and its mysterious number, 666, were understood to be hidden predictions of people or things in the present or near future, since the sincere belief of the Darbyists was that the end was almost here. In fact, every few years since 1829 these people have predicted that the "end" events would begin. (They have always been wrong but that has not diminished their zeal.)

Darby was an indefatigable worker as well as an intense zealot for this cause and system. He traveled in Europe, to New Zealand, and to the North American continent seven times between 1862 and 1877. One recalls that this first visit came during the dark days (apocalyptic times) of the Civil War. His zeal and command of Scripture texts so fascinated some American clergy that they accepted his system and became zealots for its dissemination in this country. The leader was James H. Brookes, who helped to found a summer Bible conference in 1875, the basic purpose of which was to study and propagate this system of interpretation. These conferences were held until 1897.

A young follower of Brookes, however, continued the conference on a much smaller scale in New Jersey. He had a dream of preparing a study Bible with Darbyist notes for the average layperson so as to distribute this system more widely. In 1909 his dream was realized with the publication of the *Scofield Reference Bible.* The young man was Cyrus I. Scofield. The publication of this study Bible was a most significant event. It ensured that the Darbyist system would be distributed widely and would have significant impact on Christians, especially Protestant Christians, in the United States. That is exactly what happened.

As Scofield aged and his health deteriorated, his mantle fell upon another person, Lewis Sperry Chafer. Chafer became the first president of a school that was founded for the purpose of studying and espousing the Darbyist system of interpretation. This institution became Dallas Theological Seminary. Chafer himself wrote a large amount of material from this interpretative perspective, including an 8-volume *Systematic Theology.* Other advocates have been associated with that institution, notably the John F. Walvoords (father and son) and C. C. Ryrie. They have been the more "intellectual" of the advocates of this position, but recently the primary popularizer of this system has been Hal Lindsey, a graduate of Dallas Seminary and a consistent interpreter of the Darbyist system. His works such as *The Late, Great Planet Earth* and *The Rapture: Truth or Consequences*, among others, have exerted a tremendous influence on many people. He is certainly not the only one who espouses this interpretation but is currently perhaps the most widely known and read. If one wishes to accept this system of interpretation, one is under obligation to know its origins and its presuppositions. One is also under obligation to determine honestly whether the teachings of this system are in accord with the proper and correct meaning of the biblical texts. It is one thing to believe in a system of interpretation, but it is another to impose that system on texts which originally did not mean what advocates of that system want them to mean. One must have some integrity and honesty with regard to dealing with the biblical texts.

The purpose of this study of Revelation is to attempt to allow the text of Revelation to speak for itself. If one knows the historical setting of the book and understands that it must be interpreted as an apocalyptic work, many of the misconceptions and misunderstandings will be removed. Then the intended message of the book will become rather obvious. The key is to allow the text to speak for itself. That is the simplest, best, and most honest way to deal with the teaching of Revelation. Correctly understood it carries a powerful message.

THE BOOK OF REVELATION

INTRODUCTION

The earliest tradition concerning the origin of the book of Revelation indicates that the book was written toward the end of the first century A.D. during a persecution directed against Christians in Asia Minor (present-day Turkey) by the Roman government. If that tradition is correct, the book is to be dated about A.D. 94–95. The authorship of the book has traditionally been assigned to John the apostle, and this association with John the apostle played no small part in the book's final acceptance into the formal canon of New Testament writings. The author obviously wrote to people under duress and urged them to remain loyal and faithful even in the face of persecution.

None of these ideas has gone unchallenged by critical investigation, however. The primary problem is that of authorship. The idea that John the apostle wrote the book of Revelation developed in the church and does not appear to have been an early identification of the author. It did not take long for the apostolic connection to be made since the book obviously enjoyed some popularity in the early church and since the books that were most meaningful were usually traced back to an apostle or a companion of an apostle. Some of the early church fathers who studied the book were struck by differences in style, language, vocabulary, and other matters between Revelation and the other writings attributed to John the apostle (i.e., the gospel and the three epistles). In the third century, therefore, there was already a questioning of the apostolic authorship of Revelation. If one assigns apostolic authorship to the gospel and epistles of John and finds that the authorship of Revelation is different from those writings, the authorship by John the apostle is no longer a possibility. The larger question, however, is whether the gospel and epistles are the work of the apostle! Whatever one's final disposition of that problem, it is generally agreed that Revelation was written by someone other than the writer of the gospel and epistles.

Who the author might be, if not John the apostle, has given rise to several theories. One of the most frequently heard is that which identifies a person known as John the Elder as the author of this work. From early traditions there are references to a leader of the church at Ephesus at the end of the first century known as John the Elder. Naturally this was a logical second choice if the apostle were not the author. The time, the place, and the authority of the person John the Elder would all fit into what was known about the book of Revelation and its setting.

Others have rejected the idea that John the Elder wrote the book, some even doubting the tradition of the existence of such a person at Ephesus. If the author were not John the apostle or John the Elder, who then is left? The only thing that can be known with certainty is that the author of Revelation calls himself "John" (cf. 1:4, 9; 22:8). The use of the name does not appear to be a pseudonym (though some scholars will debate that point). Whoever he is, he is known to the people in the churches to which he writes. It is obvious that he is a person of some authority, for he expects the people in the churches to heed his challenges and directives. Further, it appears that he does not consider himself to be an apostle, which would be strange if indeed he had been! What he does appear to do is to link himself to the church as a prophet. He does not call himself a prophet, but he does seem to be related to that group (cf. 1:3; 22:6, 9). There was in the early church a group of people known as "prophets" who performed certain tasks in the church, usually exhorting and challenging and teaching the community. One can see this reflected in Paul's writings, the earliest books of the New Testament to be written (cf. I Cor. 12:10, 27; 14:3-5). From an examination of the text itself, John does seem to have belonged to that group.

The final disposition of the problem of authorship has yet to be made. What is known with some certainty is that the author was a leader in the early Christian communities in the area of Asia Minor, and he seems to have been highly respected and esteemed by those people. His name was John. More than this cannot be known with the data now available to us.

Where John was when the book was written seems plain enough. He tells us that he is on the isle of Patmos (1:9) because of his witness to Jesus and his devotion to God's "word." This is certainly plausible since the Romans did banish and exile persons they deemed troublesome. These people were not to be executed, either because they had not committed any crime worthy of the death penalty or because executing them would have caused greater turmoil than simply removing them from the area. The Romans were also known to banish people because of religious problems these people posed. The place of origin for Revelation, then, seems clear enough, even though there are some who argue that John "saw" the visions on Patmos but did not actually write them down until later. This is not likely, however.

The date of John's writing has been questioned by numerous scholars. According to the early traditions and the usual consensus of scholarly opinion, the date of writing comes at the end of the first century near the end of the reign of the Roman emperor, Domitian. This would make the date about A.D. 94–95. This dating is based on the belief that Domitian reinaugurated the practice of requiring the state cultus (i.e., worship of the Roman state and thus at times the emperor) to be observed in Asia Minor. There was already there at Pergamum a temple (erected ca. 29 B.C.), which served as the center for this practice in the area of Asia Minor. According to the early traditions, Domitian was persecuting the Christians in that area, and this tradition has been supplemented by references in Roman documents to Domitian's wanting to be known as *Dominus et Deus* (Lord and God). There is also some evidence that there were in Domitian's own family some Christians whom he did not like and did away with. These thoughts coupled with the clear indication in the book of Revelation that a persecution was in fact being directed against the Christian people there by the Roman government have led most commentators to date the book around A.D. 94–95.

There is no *direct* evidence, however, that Domitian led a persecution of Christians in Asia Minor during his reign. Lack of such data has caused some

42

scholars to revise their ideas on the dating of this book. Many have sought to find where *real* persecution of the Christian community by the Roman state did, in fact, take place. There are two possibilities: (1) under Nero in Rome, around A.D. 64–66; or (2) under Trajan in Asia Minor, around A.D. 110–115. Some scholars date Revelation during the time of Nero since that persecution can be well documented. There are problems with that identification, however. To cite only a few, there is the problem with place (the persecution in Revelation is in Asia Minor not Rome) and the problem with certain historical allusions (e.g., calling Rome "Babylon," when this identification was probably not made until after A.D. 70 with the destruction of Jerusalem and the Temple by Rome).

The other date, which relates to the reign of Trajan, does indicate that the persecution is in the area of Asia Minor, but most scholars feel that the historical setting in A.D. 110–115 is later than the setting found in Revelation itself. Further, the type of persecution described in Pliny's letters to Trajan (Pliny was the Roman governor of the area) seems to be different and based on reasons different from those in Revelation. Therefore very few argue for this dating in A.D. 110–115.

Another possibility has been suggested of late based on a sociological approach to the book. While acknowledging that the historical setting is best understood as the time of Domitian but not being convinced that there is enough evidence to support the idea of an active persecution by Domitian, these scholars argue that there was not a real persecution but merely a perceived persecution. In other words, whether there was a genuine persecution or not, the Christians *thought* that they were being persecuted

This perception thus led to the writing of Revelation. Possibly there is some truth in this conjecture. After all, there is no evidence from Roman sources or Christian sources or from the book of Revelation itself that "multitudes" were being rounded up for execution. The tradition of the church, however, supported by the contents of Revelation, does indicate that some people were actually losing their lives in this period of "duress," and the author had been banished to a Roman island by the Roman government. These are not "perceptions" of persecution; they are, in fact, concrete examples of active persecution. Exactly what forms the persecution took is not known to us, but that there was some form of persecution directed against the Christians in Asia Minor seems obvious from the data.

This then raises the question of who the recipients of this book were. Clearly they are Christians, and they are living in Asia Minor as members of individual churches there. Some seem not to be experiencing the same degree of duress as others, but they are all called on to keep the faith, not to become apostate, in those difficult times.

How did the author choose to address these people with his message of challenge and hope? He did it by using the most appropriate literary vehicle available to him—an apocalypse. For about three hundred years this literary genre had served for this very purpose. John put it once again to good use in his time and setting. If the interpreter will keep in mind the apocalyptic mind-set and how that ideology was concretized in the literary style known as apocalyptic, there will be little difficulty in correctly understanding this great book.

As one studies the book of Revelation (and other

apocalyptic material in the Bible), it is imperative that a consistent apocalyptic understanding of these texts be applied so as to understand them properly. What one has previously heard, read, or thought should be placed aside, at least temporarily, so that one can hear these texts and interpret them like those who read or heard them originally. If one can begin to do this, one can begin to understand the book of Revelation aright.

COMMENTARY

Introduction (1:1-11)

The book of Revelation has two introductions. The first, verses 1-3, makes it clear that the author understands his work as an "apocalypse" (revelation). The second, verses 4-11, is an epistolary (or letter) introduction where the author identifies himself, the reason for the writing, and the recipients of this document. Revelation is, therefore, an apocalypse delivered in the form of a letter.

Vv. 1-3: After identifying his work as an apocalypse, John renders a blessing on the one who "reads the words of the prophecy." This means the one who took this document and read it in the churches for which it was intended. The author calls this apocalyptic work "prophecy." Unfortunately the popular understanding today of a prophet is that of a person who foretells and predicts the future. In the biblical materials, however, the prophet was one called by God to deliver God's message and word to God's people in a particular time and place. Predicting the future was not the primary focus of the

45

prophet's activity. The prophet sometimes did predict the future, but it was the immediate future arising directly out of the present situation. John understood his apocalypse to be God's appropriate word for the people of that time and place. The apocalyptic message was always a call for endurance in a period of persecution and a promise that the persecution would end soon. That is exactly what the author states in verse 3: "for the time is near." "Near" in the ancient world meant the same as it does now, "shortly," "soon," "in the near future." John himself clearly states that he is not speaking of distant times but of a time soon in the future when the persecution being experienced by the Christians of Asia Minor will be over. They are called on to "hear [i.e., obey] and to heed" the contents of the writing being sent.

Vv. 4-11: "John" is identified as the writer of this work. The author seems to assume that everyone will know who he is. Obviously he has some standing and some authority among these people, for he expects them to take his words seriously.

In this rather long salutation the author invokes a blessing of "grace and peace" (a rather standard Christian blessing since the time of Paul) upon his hearers and readers. It is interesting that he invokes the blessing from "the one who is and who was and is coming"; this term is John's favorite expression for God and is always used in Revelation in the nominative case (even when the grammar calls for a different case). Some commentators argue that this shows John's "sloppy" use of the Greek language, but it may be his way of asserting the unchanging and constant character of the God who is *the* hope for these Christians under persecution.

Further, there is a reference here to the "seven

spirits who are before [God's] throne." In apocalyptic the number seven designates "maturity," "fruition," thus a form of "completeness." The "seven spirits" thus refers to the "complete spirit," that is, the Holy Spirit. The last entity in the listing is that of "Jesus Christ the faithful witness." Jesus is designated as the one who was faithful to God even to the point of martyrdom, a clear call to the followers of Jesus to be similarly committed.

The call to faithful witness, however, is further defined by a continuation of the description of Jesus. Not only was he *the* faithful witness, laying down his life for God and God's work, he was also the "first-born of the dead, and the ruler of kings on earth." In spite of the very worst that the powers and forces of evil could do, Jesus triumphed over them by the power of the resurrection, which exalted him to the right hand of God and thus as ruler over the kings of the earth. Who is it who is in control? Caesar or Christ? John is certain about the answer to that question. It is to Jesus and his followers that the ultimate victory belongs. The kingdom of God is and should be the goal for all, but only those who respond positively to the invitation and who remain faithful and loyal and who do not become apostate in the face of persecution will be participants in God's kingdom and final victory.

The reference to "coming with the clouds" in verse 7 has been, naturally, taken as a reference to the return of Jesus. This is certainly one legitimate interpretation of the passage. In apocalyptic literature, however, the intervention by God or God's agent to destroy the persecutor is usually depicted by someone "coming with the clouds," a symbolic designation that when the persecution is ended God (or God's agent) is the One who will judge and remove the agent (or agents) causing the people of God to suffer. If that is the meaning here, this passage would not be a reference to Jesus' ultimate return but an explanation to the people that it will be through the intervention of God and Jesus that this period of persecution will come to its deserved end. At this stage of the book of Revelation, it is really too early to determine which of these two interpretations is intended. The reader must follow the narrative of the book to determine what the author intends.

John then identifies God as the "Alpha and Omega." These are the first and last letters of the Greek alphabet, and the figure is obviously used to point out that all of the created order and history are ultimately under the control of this magnificent Being.

At this point the author identifies himself a bit further. He appears to be known by the people for whom this book is written and seems to have some status among them. He has been exiled to the island of Patmos, a place for persons deemed troublesome in the eyes of the Roman officials. These sentences of exile could be temporary or permanent; which was John's fate he does not tell us. The interesting point here is that this apocalyptic work is not pseudonymous. Most apocalypses were written in the name of some ancient worthy of the past (e.g., Abraham, Ezra, Moses, Baruch, et al.), but this one is different. This may be the result of the fact that Christianity was a new movement and not enough time had elapsed to warrant a pseudonymous author. It may also be that the author wanted the people to know exactly who it was who was exhorting them to be faithful in this current crisis.

The author indicates that he was "in the Spirit on the Lord's day." Apocalyptic messages are usually designated as coming through spiritual revelations. Interestingly enough the emphasis here seems to be on when the revelation was given, that is, the "Lord's day," the Christian sabbath. This intensifies the message as being specifically Christian.

The destination for this revelation was "the seven churches," designated Ephesus, Smyrna, Pergamum, Thyatira, Sardis, Philadelphia, and Laodicea. The use of the number seven is typically apocalyptic, denoting all the churches affected by the persecution. These seven were selected probably because they had certain problems that were representative of all the churches involved at that time. There is no esoteric meaning in the order of the churches listed. (Some interpreters claim to have discovered in the order a hidden and symbolic history of the entire Christian church!) Why the churches are listed in this order is simple. Ephesus would be the place where someone arriving by ship would land. It was also the capital for the Roman province of Asia Minor. From Ephesus the Romans had built a road connecting other cities of the area, and this road was used by travelers and as a postal route. Once a person left Ephesus and followed this road, the cities to be visited were in the exact order found in John's listing. There is nothing strange or esoteric about that.

Part I: Son of Man Vision (1:12-20)

Vv. 12-20: The reader now encounters the first of John's apocalyptic visions. This one is rather foundational for the following section (chs. 2–3) and establishes the authority and superiority of the one

49

who is described in the vision, namely, the *Son of man*. This term was used frequently as a title for Jesus in the Gospel accounts. (Interestingly it is not found in other New Testament writings except for one reference in Acts [7:56] and in the book of Revelation.) The vision described here of the Son of man standing in the midst of his churches was designed to demonstrate to those under persecution that they were not alone in their ordeal. The One who had experienced similar animosity and who had triumphed over it was alive and well in their midst.

The seven golden lampstands represent the seven churches. In Judaism the seven-pronged candelabra, the menorah, had come to represent the Jewish people in the Graeco-Roman world. One is reminded of the arch of Titus in Rome commemorating the Roman victory over the Jewish people in Palestine in the A.D. 66–70 War. In that arch the central item appears to be the menorah. John, interestingly enough, has continued to use the candlestick as a symbol of God's people, but in his presentation there are seven individual lampstands instead of one with seven prongs. The meaning of the number seven in apocalyptic thought, however, indicates that John is really addressing all the churches, not simply these seven.

The description of the Son of man in this vision is quite detailed. He has a long robe, eyes as of fire, feet like burnished bronze, and so on. The commentators differ in their interpretations here. Some argue that each part of the description represents some aspect or characteristic of this Being, but others contend that in such an apocalyptic vision the details are accumulated to add brilliance, weight, and authority to the scene. Good arguments can be marshaled for either position. In apocalyptic imagery, however, one must be careful not to force meanings onto every detail of a visionary scene. That comes dangerously close to transforming symbolic imagery into allegory. (An allegory is a wisdom story in which every detail in the account has a hidden meaning.) The intent of the apocalyptic scene is to overwhelm the hearer (or reader) with the majesty and the magnitude of the One described. This scene was not intended to be seen with the physical eye; its purpose was to impress the spiritual dimension of those who heard.

In verses 17-20 there is the usual apocalyptic explanation of what has been described. The identity of the Son of man (in case there ever was any doubt) is made clear. He is the One who died but was not held by death. This feat gives him power over death and the place of death (Hades, not hell). It is Christ who really determines who lives or dies, not Caesar. It is Christ who has conquered evil, and therefore death. The seven stars are described as the "angels of the seven churches." In apocalyptic thought each nation (or group or sometimes even persons) had a guardian angel. The seven lampstands are identified as "the seven churches." There can be little doubt about the correct understanding of the vision. The Christian communities in Asia Minor can take heart because the real guarantor of life is in their midst and has already won the ultimate battle of death vs. life. There is no need to fear the worst that the powers and forces of evil have to offer. The One to whom Christians have committed their loyalty is with them in these difficult times—and beyond!

Part II: Letters to the Seven Churches (Chapters 2–3)

Chapters 2–3 contain a series of letters written to the specific churches mentioned in 1:11. These are real letters to real churches with real needs. There is a pattern or form, which is followed in each letter. First there is a command to write to the church, and the description of the one sending the message is given by citing certain aspects from the vision of the Son of man in 1:12-16. (It is at this point that interpreters feel most strongly that there are specific meanings to be attached to these attributes because in most instances the meaning of the attribute is very appropriate to the specific church and its situation.)

Second, the church is congratulated and commended on what it is doing right, especially in the midst of the persecution. Third, the author chastises the church for its failures and shortcomings since persecution does not justify any laxity in Christian living or commitment. In fact greater care is needed because one's life under fire can demonstrate what the real character of a person or group is. The last component in each letter is a challenge to keep the faith and a promise of reward if that is done. Since each church is different, each letter reflects the situation in its own particular setting.

2:1-7: The first letter is addressed to the church at Ephesus, or more precisely to the "angel" at that church. Since the angel is understood as a guardian angel, this appears to be somewhat peculiar. Therefore some argue that the angel could be understood as a corporate embodiment of the church or the means of revelation to the church. Further, some interpreters have understood the angel in chapters 2–3 as the leader of the church addressed since "angel" can also mean "messenger" and thus perhaps indicate a leader. Such views are not likely. Writing to the guardian angel would be understood as the same as writing directly to the church in apocalyptic symbolism. However the angel is interpreted would not really alter the understanding of the message to each church.

The characteristics of the Son of man highlighted for this church are "the one who holds the seven stars in his right hand" and "who walks among the golden lampstands." By this connection the author has emphasized that the one speaking to the church at Ephesus is the One who is Lord of and present with the church. The church owes its existence to this Son of man.

The commendation for these people is high. They have borne up well under the persecution and have been intent on keeping their number "pure," testing and removing those who were not truly committed to the cause. Their chastisement arises from this same activity. In their zeal for purity, the people have lost their sensitivity, their "love" (i.e., care and concern) for people. A self-righteous attitude had arisen or was in danger of emerging among the church's members, and it threatened their very existence as a church. There is, after all, a thin line between faithfulness to a position or cause and hypocritical spite. Obviously the people at Ephesus were too close to that line. They are warned that if they do not repent, the Son of man will come (obviously not here a reference to *the* return of Jesus) and remove their lampstand. In other words, without love they cannot be a part of the church.

The seer also commends them on their watchfulness toward the "Nicolaitans." Exactly who these people were is still a mystery, but several conjectures have been espoused. Irenaeus, an early Church Father (ca. A.D. 180), identified these people with Nicolaus of Antioch (cf. Acts 6:5) who, according to tradition, became a gnostic. Whether this identification can be accepted is a matter of debate, but many scholars do feel that these Nicolaitans (also mentioned in Rev. 2:13) were a gnostic group.

Gnosticism as a full-blown movement did not really emerge until later, but its roots are located in Greek thought-patterns of earlier times. Simply put, many of the Greeks believed that the world was divided into two spheres, spiritual and material. The spiritual was basically good, the material basically evil. In each human being there was a spark of the purely spiritual, which longed to be reunited with God, pure spirit, but it was unable to do so because it was trapped in the physical (evil) world of matter. Somehow, the knowledge (*gnosis*) of how to journey through the labyrinthine structure that separates pure spirit from the created world had been imparted to a selected few, who could share this saving "knowledge." Whoever had this knowledge could then be reunited with pure spirit upon death, the spirit being released from its physical "prison."

Once one received this knowledge, that person became a "pneumatikos," a "spiritual" being. This meant that the person was no longer in the same relationship with the world as before. Usually the "saved" gnostic would react in one of two ways, either becoming ascetic and withdrawing as much as possible from the world or ignoring the morals and mores of the world and doing anything and everything, anywhere, anytime! This thinking was not left at the "church door" when these people who were reared in that ideology became Christians. Paul, for example, in the early beginnings of the church in the larger Graeco-Roman world, had to struggle against these attitudes (cf. I Cor. 6:12-20 for one illustration of the "libertine" view, and I Cor. 7:1-6 as illustrative of the ascetic perspective). In each of the settings in Revelation when Nicolaitans are mentioned, these patterns seem to be explicit in the context, usually the libertine (which was and is always the most popular view).

The challenge to the church at Ephesus is to "conquer," that is, to remain faithful in the time of persecution and to keep the faith without losing that ingredient essential for a church, namely, love. The promise is that those who do will be rewarded by knowing that their legacy will never be overcome but will continue (they will eat of the tree of life in the paradise of God).

2:8-11: The attributes of the Son of man lifted out for the church at Smyrna are directed toward the ultimate triumph of life. There were in Smyrna obviously those who were persecuting the Christians most grievously. There is a reference to *Jews* here aiding in the persecution. Whether there were really Jews or whether the author is using the term to refer to any who opposed the church and those who were continuing the work of Christ is open to question. It is true, however, that there was a strong cadre of Jewish people in Smyrna, and we know that not long after the writing of Revelation these people were heavily involved in the martyrdom of a church leader, Polycarp. According to Eusebius the Jews collected timber for the burning of Polycarp even though it was the Sabbath (cf. Eusebius, *Ecclesiastical History*, 13:1).

Whoever the perpetrators, there is a definite threat here of explicit persecution. This would last for "ten days," in apocalyptic jargon, a completed period of time. If the people will be faithful, even to

death, they will be rewarded with "the crown of life."
Further, they will not be harmed by the "second
death." This is the first mention of the "second death"
in Revelation. Exactly what it is, John does not
explain at this point, but it is clear from the context
that it is a death over and above the first death, the
physical death all humans experience.

In the biblical writings physical death does not
seem to be a curse; rather it is a part of the natural
order of creation. The second death, however, is
something very different, and this death is to be
dreaded and feared. Whatever it is, those who remain
faithful and loyal to God and Christ will not be hurt
by this phenomenon.

2:12-17: The church at Pergamum seems to be a
mixed group, some being faithful and others in need
of some repentance. Thus the characteristic of the
Son of man directed to this group is the "two-edged
sword," a "word" that protects the faithful but
punishes the unfaithful.

This church was located in the very center of the
cult of Rome and the Emperor. There was a temple
there which had been dedicated to Rome and the
emperor Augustus in 29 B.C. When the new emphasis
on the veneration of the state and its ruler was
reemphasized, it was only natural that this place
would be the focal point for that worship (thus the
reference to "Satan's throne"). At least one person,
Antipas, had been martyred already and further
persecution seems to have been imminent.

Nevertheless, in spite of these difficult circumstances, the church was expected to uphold proper
actions with regard to their Christian faith. The
people at Pergamum, therefore, are chastised for
improper behavior. Some of this was obviously

related to gnostic belief, primarily of the libertine type. The reference to Balaam has caused some confusion among interpreters. Balaam was the person hired by the king of Moab (Balak) to curse Israel as that people crossed through the land on their way to Canaan (cf. Numbers 22–24). The use of Balaam as a symbol here is usually understood by interpreters to refer to corrupt and improper teaching, which would prove to be harmful to the people of God. Balaam had become the symbolic embodiment of all false teachers. For those who were falling prey to this false teaching, which led inevitably to immoral living, there is a stern warning (v. 16).

The promise for those who keep the faith is interesting. They are to receive the "hidden manna" and a "white stone." There are numerous interpretations of these figures. The most likely possibility for the manna is to understand it as a reference to the new manna, which was to descend from heaven when the new age comes. Such an idea and figure are found in another apocalyptic work, II Baruch (29:8). This symbol is obviously derived from the life-giving and life-sustaining manna of the Exodus accounts.

This figure is coupled here with that of a "white stone," something obviously having to do with victory. Again there are numerous theories about this figure. In the ancient world a white stone was sometimes used as the ticket for admission into a certain society, group, or other association. Here it seems to carry that same connotation, admission to God's new age freed from the hardships of persecution. The reference to the "new name . . . which no one knows" is to be understood against the ancient idea that to know someone's name gave a person a certain power over the person whose name was known. To have a name that "no one knows" indicates that only the one who gave the name (in this case, God) and the person the name is given to have any power or control over that person's destiny. Here is a clear call for ultimate commitment in the face of demonic persecution at the very center of that evil.

2:18-29: The letter to Thyatira is the longest of all the seven, in spite of the fact that this city was the smallest and least influential of all the cities addressed. The attributes from the vision in chapter 1 include the "eyes of fire" and the "feet of burnished bronze," again indicating that the Son of man sees beneath the surface and judges accordingly.

The people are commended for their works and patient endurance, but there is also a strong element of immorality in the church (again probably of the gnostic type). This immorality was led by a woman, Jezebel. Whether this was her real name or whether the name was selected because of similarities with the Jezebel from Kings who led the people into idolatry (cf. I Kings 16ff.), one is unable to say. Numerous identifications have been suggested for this woman (one even being that she was the wife of the "bishop" there!), but the primary consideration is her leading the church people astray. The clearly sexual imagery may be indicative of that type of problem in the church, but imagery depicting sexual immorality is also frequently used for idolatry and false worship. In fact, many scholars argue that the problem in Thyatira resided in the association of the Christians there with the powerful trade guilds, which were dedicated usually to one of the foreign gods.

The reference to the "deep things of Satan" may

argue for gnostic influence since later gnostics liked to talk about "deep things." Those who are led astray by these evils will be "devastated with a rod of iron." The Greek term has led to two translations of this verse (27) as "shepherd with a rod of iron" (KJV) or "rule with a rod of iron" (RSV), and both are misleading. From the Semitic background the word *to shepherd* came to have various nuances, one of which was to destroy, devastate. The context here seems to call for that meaning. It is interesting to note that those who "overcome" will be wielding "power over the nations." The ultimate victory belongs to God and to those who remain faithful to God. This is further emphasized by the reference, "I will give him the morning star" (v. 28). This term is found in numerous apocalyptic works usually to indicate the reward and glory the victor in this cosmic struggle of good versus evil would receive (cf. Dan. 12:3; II Esdras 7:97). Later Jesus is designated the morning star. If that connection is intended here, the meaning would be that the victory already won by the Christ (cf. 1:5, 18) will be passed along to and shared by the faithful followers in those evil times.

3:1-6: Here is the "worst" church of the seven. It has the semblance of life but is really dead. Accordingly, the attributes of the visionary being from chapter 1 emphasize the enlivening activity of God's spirit in the church and God's protection of the church. The problem with this group seems to be a lack of vigilance. They never complete (v. 2) their works and are asleep. Such should not have been the case in any church but especially not in Sardis. This was a city situated on a hill, a veritable impregnable fortress if properly guarded. It had however, because of a lack of watchfulness, fallen to invasion in its history.

There were a few persons individually who had kept the faith, but the church as an entity in itself was dead. There is a reference to names being written in a book, a typical apocalyptic figure denoting security and assurance for those under persecution. This security is not unconditional, however, because names could be blotted out of the book. Faithfulness has to be constant and continuous if one is to remain a part of God's church and elect. The ones who remain faithful will ultimately be victorious and have a place before God in the final accounting.

3:7-13: Philadelphia is a church commended for its steadfastness in the face of fierce opposition from those outside the Christian community. For this reason the attributes of the Son of man directed to these people are truth (i.e., reality, genuineness) and the power to "open and shut" (i.e., to control ultimate destiny in the face of persecution).

There were opportunities for work and witness open to these people, and no outside opposition could keep anyone who wanted to bear witness to the faith from doing so. The two verb forms in verse 8, "I have set" (Greek "given") and "open" (a participle), are both perfect tenses indicating an action completed with the results continuing on to the present. The opportunity to witness has been and will continue to be open for those who will do that. The opposition here comes from a "synagogue [or assembly] of Satan." Whether these are to be identified with a Jewish community in Philadelphia or whether the term is to be understood figuratively cannot be determined with certainty. What is clear is that these collaborators with evil will see the ultimate victory of the people of God. The people are urged to hold on (v. 11) because "I am coming soon." What this coming is exactly to be has not as yet been established, but here it seems to emphasize that the persecution will soon be over.

The promise to those who remain loyal is that they will be made "pillars in the temple of my God." There are again several theories on the exact origin of this figure, no one of which seems to have gained common acceptance. Nevertheless, the figure is clear in its meaning—the faithful ones will become permanent components of God's temple and will dwell in the presence of God always. They will share God's "name," probably a reference again to security since God's ultimate triumph is linked with God's essence and being. There is a reference also to the "new Jerusalem," which is not defined or explained here. That larger explanation will come in chapter 21 (see part IX, pp. 119-22).

3:14-22: The reader now comes to the last of the seven letters to the churches, last because Laodicea is the final stop on the road from Ephesus. Some have argued that this is the "worst" of the churches, but it seems to be neither worse nor better than most of the others. (Obviously the "worst," if one wishes to arrange these churches in such categories, would have to be Sardis, which was "dead.")

This church was situated in the midst of an important and wealthy city. Laodicea was an important commercial center with strong interests in banking, textile manufacturing, and medicine with an emphasis on "eye salve," which was purported to have healing qualities. Interestingly enough this city did not always have a water supply of its own, which meant that water had to be piped in from some distance. The nearest available supply was from a hot springs; thus, when the water arrived it was lukewarm. All of these factors are used by John in his note to this church. Here was a church that was basically self-sufficient and obviously self-satisfied. Thus the characteristics of the Son of man applied here refer to the steadfast and genuine witness to God's purposes and emphasize that God can make things new through the process of their keeping the faith and allowing God's Spirit to continue its creative work in the church.

Using a figure the people of Laodicea could certainly understand, John compares the church to tepid water, which is potentially good but in its tepid state is a bit sickening! The problem is self-satisfaction with who, what, and where they are. Thinking that they are rich, well-clothed, and have the right medicine to "see" properly, the people in the church here are in danger of being spiritually poor, naked, and blind. Again the challenge is, as it was to other churches, to reaffirm commitment to God and Christ since that commitment often means "chastening," at this time in the form of persecution.

Verses 20-22 are debated somewhat among interpreters. Most think that they are the conclusion to the letter to Laodicea, thus making each of the letters self-contained and ending with a call for "all the churches" to pay attention to the message directed toward that particular church. Other interpreters argue that these verses are a summary of the messages to all the churches. Either interpretation is possible but it seems to be more likely that the letter is a unity as the others are, and since each letter concludes with a call for "the churches" to pay heed to what has been said to each one, it is not likely that this letter lacks its own particular conclusion. Further, since there is no general introduction to the letters as a whole, there seems to be no need to find a general conclusion.

It is interesting to note that this passage (vv. 20-22) has frequently been used by evangelists to urge persons to "open their hearts to the Jesus who knocks" on the door of human hearts. In the context here, however, it is not the door of the individual's heart but the church door on which Jesus is rapping. The idea seems to be that the church by apostasy, apathy, immorality, and so on, can shut Jesus out of his own church. Some individuals may indeed hear and respond, but it is the church at large which is central here. The ones who remain faithful will be with God and Christ, participants in the victory of good over the powers and forces of evil.

These seven letters contain challenges, exhortations, and warnings for the churches caught up in the social and political forces of that time and place. The people are encouraged to keep the faith and are promised that they will share in the same victory that was demonstrated in and through the life, death, and resurrection of the church's Lord. This is a typical apocalyptic message even though the section itself is not in the form of an apocalyptic vision but rather presented as letters to the churches addressed in this book.

Part III: Vision of God and the Lamb (Chapters 4–5)

From this point on in the book of Revelation, the author presents only apocalyptic visions. Each is essentially self-contained and intended to present certain aspects of the author's message to the churches. Even though each vision is separate the author has done a masterful job of interweaving images and figures looking back and ahead so as to present a "unified" literary work. In these visionary scenarios John uses typical apocalyptic images and symbols, but he also makes use of a large number of figures and scenes from the Old Testament (which was, after all, his Bible). Some of these figures are very significant, and one cannot but notice the author's use of numerous Old Testament texts.

The magnificent vision of chapters 4–5 depicts the reason for John's confidence and why he feels that it is so important to keep the faith and not fall away from it.

*4:1-6*a: The scene is typical of apocalyptic visions. The author is transported to the heavenly place to view something special, something "revealed." In this episode, that which is revealed is nothing less than a glimpse into the very throne room of God. The one sitting on the throne is never specifically described, only the splendor of the majesty. The scene is set with precious stones similar to our quartz or rock crystal (i.e., the jasper, carnelian, and perhaps the emerald also), which naturally refract light. Obviously there will be a resultant rainbow, a reminder to the Christian people of the God of the covenant who had made a promise not to destroy the people again (cf. Gen. 9:8-17). Herein is their hope, to set their trust in this magnificent Being.

Around (i.e., in the presence of) the One seated on the throne were twenty-four smaller thrones and on them were twenty-four "elders." There have been numerous suggestions about the identity of these elders, ranging from glorified human beings to angelic beings of various sorts. Some have found mythological or zodiacal prototypes for this figure. The exact origin of the figure is not really important, however. In the apocalyptic context the white garments and golden crowns indicate that there are those who have "won the victory," that is, they have fought the fight of faith in the face of persecution and triumphed. The fact that there are twenty-four is significant in that the number is a multiple of twelve, indicating the people of God. Some interpreters argue that the 24 (2 x 12) includes the representatives of God's faithful people, both from old Israel and from the new people of God, the church. All the faithful from God's people from all ages are here in the very presence of God, where the Spirit of God dwells (the seven torches of fire represent God's Spirit; cf. 1:4). They have been loyal in the struggle against evil.

The sea of glass before the throne is a figure probably taken from throne rooms of ancient times, where the king sat upon a throne on a raised platform. The area in front of the throne was usually made of polished marble or some other highly reflective material. In this scene the sea of glass simply adds to the intensity of the light and magnifies the splendor of the entire setting. Obviously this vision was never intended to be viewed with the human eye, but to be seen with the spiritual eye.

4:6b-11: The vision continues with the description of four living creatures (a figure taken from Ezekiel 1–2). In the thinking of that time, the created order was divided into four categories: wild beasts, domesticated animals, human beings, and birds. Each was represented by an animal characteristic of the group, the wild beasts by a lion, domesticated animals by an ox, humans by a human, and birds by an eagle. (Later these four were attached to the four gospels, but that was not the intent here.) The meaning is that God's glory is, in part, supported by the created order, and God's sovereignty is supreme over that order. The description of these four creatures blends the Ezekiel passage and aspects of the call of Isaiah (cf. Isaiah 6), where the seraphim have six wings each. The song sung before the throne is also derived from the Isaiah passage.

All the components in the vision, the living creatures and the elders, participate in unceasing praise to the One who is Lord over all creation. They sing a hymn of praise in which they emphasize God's sovereignty over the created order: "By your will they [i.e., 'all things'] came into being and were fashioned into what they are" (v. 11, paraphrase).

5:1-10: The scene remains the same, but now the focus has shifted to another figure. The seer notices in the right hand of God a scroll inscribed on both sides (another figure from Ezekiel) that has been sealed with seven seals. Exactly what the scroll contains has been a source of debate. Is it a will, or the revelation of God in the Bible (i.e., Old Testament), or a description of the history of the world, or an outline of the *end,* or God's plan of redemption? All these theories and more have been suggested. In the context of the book, however, it appears that the scroll was the unfolding of God's judgment on the ones who were persecuting God's people at that moment of history. This would be a typical apocalyptic use and seems to fit the context best of all the theories.

A search was made for someone "worthy" to open the scroll. Interestingly enough it is not power that is at issue but rather value. There is drama here in that no one was found who was worthy in heaven or on earth or under the earth (i.e., anyone who had ever lived). Then the seer is told not to be sorrowful for the "Lion of the tribe of Judah, . . . the Root of David" could open the scroll. Both of these terms were used for the expected Messiah, who was understood to be God's agent to lead the armies of God against the enemies of God's people in establishing a new age. The emphasis was on raw power. The focus then shifts to the center of the scene where John describes not a marauding lion but a lamb, and not simply a lamb but a lamb that had been slaughtered! The value system of God is quite different, obviously, from that of humankind. God's purposes are to be accomplished through a sacrificial lamb. This lamb, even though it has been slain, nevertheless stands— it has overcome the indignity and power of death. A horn in apocalyptic usually designates power, and an eye, wisdom or insight. This lamb has seven horns and seven eyes indicating that it has complete power and complete wisdom. This power and wisdom have been sent into the earth via the "seven spirits" (i.e., the Holy Spirit), a standard teaching of the early church.

The lamb then takes the scroll from God. This act sets off another scene of worship and praise with a hymn that emphasizes the Messiah's sacrifice so that people from all the earth may be redeemed and become a part of God's new people (in verse 10, "a kingdom [even] priests to our God"). It is God's will to give these people a share in the ultimate victory.

5:11-14: The entire vision now concludes with all those beings who are allied with God and Christ singing out majestically hymns of praise, honor, and glory to those two figures. In verse 12 one notes that there are seven ascriptions of praise the slain lamb receives. The scene concludes with all the beings worshiping and ascribing praise to God as an act of gratitude and thanksgiving.

Part IV: The Cycle of the Seven Seals (Chapter 6)

Before moving into the text of the cycle of the seven seals, it is well to discuss this and the two other numbered cycles (of the seven trumpets, 8:1–11:19, and of the seven bowls, chs. 15–16). There has been some confusion in the history of the interpretation of Revelation about these three cycles, and two ways of viewing them have vied for acceptance. Early in the history of the church, these cycles were understood in a "historical-continuous" manner. That means that the three were understood to depict three separate scenes, which would occur within history and would follow one another in the same sequence as they are presented in Revelation.

There are, however, some real problems with understanding the cycles in this way. For example, each one seems to be in a sense self-contained. The cycle of the seven trumpets, for example, specifically states at its conclusion that "the kingdom of the world has become the kingdom of our Lord and of his Christ, and he shall reign for ever and ever" (11:15). What else could possibly be needed past this? Yet the narrative continues. This set of circumstances led to another approach to the interpretation of these cycles, namely the "recapitulation" method. The idea here is that since each of the cycles seems to be self-contained and conclusive in itself, they are simply three different ways of describing the same scenario, each being a recapitulation of the other. This approach emerged early in the church's struggle with making sense out of the marvelous yet disturbing book of Revelation.

Although many accepted this approach to the three cycles, there were still unanswered questions. Why are there three of those scenes if nothing is really added by including all of them? How does one explain the differences among the three? For example, in the cycle of the seven seals only one fourth is judged; in the cycle of the seven trumpets, one third is judged; but in the cycle of the seven bowls, the reader is told that this is "the last" and that "all" (of a certain group) are judged. Surely something must have been intended by the author with regard to these differences.

If one will recall that apocalyptic writings consist basically of a series of self-contained visionary units, there is really no problem. Each scene is intended to teach something to the people addressed about their situation and to offer some hope in the midst of that predicament. In the context of the book of Revelation, it appears that these three do have something to teach about the nature of evil and God's judgment on it and its cohorts. If this is true, then there is no problem other than learning what each of the visions has to say. Problems relating to chronological sequence are imported into the text because the nature of apocalyptic has not been fully understood.

6:1-8: Perhaps the most famous of the figures in the book of Revelation is that of the four horsemen. These mysterious riders are found in this cycle of the seven seals and form a significant part of the scene. Needless to say there have been numerous interpretations of these riders and their steeds, ranging from identification of persons and events in Roman history (before A.D. 90), to mythological characters, to predictions of persons and events to come in the future when the "end-times" begin. It would take too long to discuss all these theories, and that is not really our purpose in this study. If one recalls that this is one of the apocalyptic scenes, arising out of that specific historical situation, it is not really difficult to ascertain the meaning of the vision.

The lamb opens the first of the seals, and one of the living creatures thunders, "Come out!" What appears is a rider on a white horse who goes out "conquering and for the purpose of conquering" (v. 2). Since the rider sits upon a white horse, many have wrongly assumed that this must be the Messiah. White in apocalyptic, however, is primarily a symbol of victory, and the description of the rider makes it clear that a conqueror is intended here, but the identity of the rider is disputed. Some interpreters have identified him as the king of the Parthians (Parthia was the successor nation to old Persia), some as the personification of the agent of evil, among other possibilities. If one places oneself in the position of those persons for whom this book was originally intended, the identity of the rider seems fairly obvious. The horseman is one who has set out to impose his will on any and all who oppose him. To the Christians in Asia Minor, this could only mean one person—the Roman emperor Domitian.

When such a situation arises, that is, when someone imposes restrictions and demands obedience over and above ordinary restraint for the good of a community, consequences will naturally ensue. The three following horsemen represent, then, the stages of those consequences. The second horse is red, the apocalyptic symbol for war or strife, and the rider brandishes a sword and takes "peace from the earth." Unless all people acquiesce to the will of a conqueror, the natural consequence is war, strife, or conflict. This conflict then leads to difficult times, described here by the black horse and its rider. Black symbolizes the lack of something, in this instance food. From other places in the book of Revelation, it seems that one of the primary weapons used against the Christian community was exclusion from the marketplace, economic leverage to force the apostasy of those who resisted. Here, the symbol of famine makes that quite clear. A quart of wheat (v. 6) would keep one person alive for one day; a denarius was a day's wage. What would happen to a family in such a setting? Further, barley was usually looked upon as food for the poor and outcasts; the people who resisted had been reduced to those categories. The availability of the "oil and wine" is probably a reference to the fact that only those who opposed the one on the white horse were deprived of daily essentials. Others had access to what was needed.

After the strife and the lack of normal situations, the end result of forcing one's will on others issues in the fourth horseman, the rider on the "pale" horse. The word translated "pale" is in the Greek *chloros,* which means "greenish gray," the color of a corpse. The rider is identified as Death, and the "place of the dead" (i.e., Hades) follows in their wake ("Hades" does not mean hell but rather the place of the dead). With this horseman the cycle is complete. The one who goes out "conquering and for the purpose of conquering" sets into motion a sequence of events that leads through conflict and harsh times, and issues in death. Though it is not explicitly stated in the text, the meaning seems to be that persons from both sides are involved in the consequences of the cycle.

6:9-11: Most important for the author and his hearers are those who are martyred for the cause, in this case the cause of Christ and his church. The fifth seal shifts the scene from earth to heaven, where there are seen those who "had been slain for the word of God and for the witness they had borne." What about those people who had given the "last full measure of devotion" for the cause of Christ? Typical of every apocalyptic work the author indicates that these people are already in a special place reserved for them in heaven, under the very altar of God. There is always a special reward for martyrs. There is also a clear call for continued resistance to the powers of evil and a conviction that the end of the persecution, although it may be near, is not over and will require more martyrs.

There are some people who are "turned off" by apocalyptic writings because in such works the persecuted (both alive and martyred) cry out for justice. Many do not feel that it is appropriate for Christians to "seek vengeance," but such a view is somewhat distorted. In the first place these martyrs have already given their lives, are already enjoying the rewards for their faithfulness, and have nothing to gain from the enemies' destruction. Their loved ones and Christian sisters and brothers may, but their own cry is not primarily selfish. Second, their cry agrees with the nature and will of God, that is, *for* righteousness and *in opposition to* evil and its powers. What they want is God's will and justice to be done, not revenge for themselves. Finally, they understand the full significance of the struggle being waged. It is, in typical apocalyptic ideology, the acknowledgment of the cosmic, to-the-death, struggle of good versus evil, of God versus Satan and the powers of darkness. The martyrs' cry is for God to act so that the victory of good will prevail. If God does not act, the powers and forces of evil will triumph and all hope for humanity and the universe will vanish. Is it really out of step with the teachings of Jesus to want Satan and the forces of evil to be destroyed? The apocalyptists think not.

6:12-17: To this point in the cycle, the reader or hearer has been introduced to what comes about when someone, mad with power, attempts to impose that person's agenda on all others. There is a series of events inaugurated, which runs its course and ultimately issues in death. This death does not include only the death of those who ally themselves with such evil but the death of those who oppose it as well. The fifth seal indicates, however, that those who resist evil and suffer martyrdom will have a very special reward.

Even though evil is partially self-destructive (the basic teaching of the four horsemen), the full judgment on evil is certain because God has willed that those who ally themselves with evil will receive their just reward. The sixth seal indicates this very clearly. In apocalyptic literature God's judgment on evil is frequently depicted as accompanied by aberrations of nature. Since God was the ruler over the created order, any dramatic deviation in nature was interpreted as a sign of God's intervention, in this case for the judgment on evil. It is interesting to note here (and later also) that the judgment does not come upon the entire created order or upon all people, but rather the judgment falls on those who have allied themselves with the forces of evil in this period of persecution against the people of God.

The scene depicted in this sixth seal is very similar to some found in the prophetic books, especially

Amos (cf. Amos 8:9-10; 9:2-4). The clear teaching is that no one who deserves God's judgment can escape it, not even by hiding in obscure places. The grave tragedy is that God's judgment is so dreadful that the people cry out for the mountains to fall on them to escape that most horrible moment! God's justice may sometimes seem slow, but it is indeed certain.

An Interlude (Chapter 7)

At this juncture the reader may feel that the last seal is to be opened and that whatever final conclusion is to be made will be made. Interestingly enough the sixth seal is in a real sense the end of the cycle of the seven seals, for out of the seventh seal another cycle of seven arises. Even though the reader now anticipates the seventh seal, the author has inserted an "interlude" between the sixth and seventh seals. This interlude depicts the "sealing" of the people of God. In this context the act of sealing indicates God's special protection upon those who remain faithful and do not become apostate. This does not mean that each individual person will be protected and none will be martyred. It does mean, however, that God will protect the group and that the group will indeed survive and continue after the persecution is over. This interlude is divided into sections.

7:1-8: As always there are several problems and differences of opinion with regard to the proper interpretation of this passage. The identity of the 144,000 who are sealed and the listing of the individual tribes are perhaps the two most debated issues. First, however, there is really no mystery about why the author used the number 144,000. It is a typical apocalyptic figure composed of a multiple of 10 (completeness) and a multiple of 12 (the people of God). The 144,000 represent the totality of the people of God. There is no thought here of 144,000 individuals and not one more!

A more substantial problem is that of the specific identity of those 144,000. Since they are said to be from the "tribes of Israel," many have understood them to be Jewish Christians, in other words, Christians who were formerly Jews. This seems not to be likely since the people addressed were surely a mixed group of Christians who were from both the Jewish *and* Gentile worlds. Others have argued that these refer to a group of Jewish people who will sometime in the future become part of the Christian community. This also seems unlikely since the people being described here seem to be directly addressed; that is, they are the community being persecuted at that moment of history. Others have argued that these 144,000 represent a select group from within the church at that time who will survive the persecution. It appears from the context and in the light of usual apocalyptic methodology that this group represents the entire people of God, and the promise (by "sealing," i.e., protecting) is that the people of God will indeed survive both the persecution and the judgment on the persecutors.

There are some interpreters who see in the listing of the twelve tribes a hidden symbolism. For example, since the Messiah was to come from the tribe of Judah, that tribe was mentioned first. Further, there is an intertestamental work (*The Testaments of the Twelve Patriarchs*), which talks about some being or person who opposes the work of

the Messiah. This one was to come from the tribe of
Dan (cf. *Testament of Dan*, 5:6-7; 6:1). Since that idea
was known in the time of John's writing of
Revelation, some argue that he chose not to include
Dan in the listing of the tribes so as not to give any
possible indication that evil could come from within
the people of God.

Once more, these are interesting ideas and could
possibly be correct, but the overall meaning of the
passage is very clear without these understandings
imposed on the text. Further, to press the order and
listing of the tribes for theological purposes seems to
be somewhat dubious. After all, there are in the Old
Testament twenty different arrangements and list-
ings of the tribes! The sealing of the 144,000 (the
people of God) clearly teaches that in spite of the
persecution God will protect and defend the community so that it will survive.

7:9-17: The second part of the interlude shifts
from the earthly community to the heavenly realm.
Here is answered the question of what happens to
those who are martyred in the persecution. The
earthly group will survive, but what about those
faithful persons who give their lives for the cause?
The scene is reminiscent of that in chapter 4, but
here those who have won the final victory ("clothed
in white robes") take their place around God's
throne along with all those who have been faithful
and loyal throughout all generations, a multitude
that cannot be numbered! The emphasis, of course,
is on those who have given their lives in this present
"persecution" (the proper translation of "tribulation"). These take their place before God and learn
what their faithfulness has made secure for them
(vv. 15-17).

The Book of Revelation

Part V: The Cycle of the Seven Trumpets
(8:1–11:19)

The interlude is now over. The reader or hearer can anticipate the opening of the seventh seal. Surprisingly, instead of an "end" to the drama with the opening of this seal, there arises instead a new cycle of seven. Some interpreters have found little to commend this cycle. It is not as dramatic or memorable as either the seven seals or the seven bowls (yet to come in chapters 15–16). If one understands that each of these apocalyptic visions contains teachings and ideas the author wishes to present and that each of the visions is in a real sense self-contained, then one can search for the intended meaning rather than compare the three to see which is better stated.

Obviously the cycle of the seven seals teaches something about the persecution. Although the cycle of the seven seals showed that evil was self-destructive even while imposing its will on God's people, the cycle of the seven trumpets shows that nature itself is also involved in judgment. Since God is the One who controls the natural order, any deviation in that order such as described here indicates that God is an active participant in this judgment. When evil is unleashed and uncontrolled the natural order can turn from its role of defender and sustainer of life to a destructive force. This happens because God can and does intervene in the continuing processes of nature and history.

The interpreter finds once again in this cycle a rather long interlude, between the sixth and seventh trumpet. This interlude teaches essentially the same lessons as the interlude between the sixth and seventh seals, but in very different imagery and with different emphases.

Ch. 8: The short period of silence at the opening of the seventh seal has long puzzled interpreters. Is this "silence" an indicator of a lull before a large battle, an allusion to primordial silence before creation, or simply a dramatic pause in the continuing literary saga the apocalyptist describes? There is little agreement at this point among commentators, but it seems that the third option is the simplest and may well be correct. The drama is heightened by this silence.

At this point the angels blow the trumpets and a new sequence of episodes begins. These episodes are filled with typical apocalyptic symbolism and imagery, and it seems best to understand the first four as a kind of unity (cf. the first four seals). The reader is struck almost immediately by the images and figures. They are obviously borrowed from the story of the Exodus and the plagues associated with that momentous event in the history of God's ancient people (cf. Exod. 7:20–12:32). The teaching is clear: God can and does intervene directly to assist God's persecuted people. One notes again that the judgment is partial (here "one third").

9:1-12: With the scenario of the fifth trumpet, the scene switches from earth to a glimpse of a spiritual scene—this time from the demonic side. What is described is a hideous array of locusts, which ascend to the earth from the jaws of hell. They were unleashed by a "fallen star." Is this star to be understood as the leader of the powers and forces of evil or as a human representative of that realm? Interpreters are divided, but again it seems that the teaching of the apocalyptist emphasizes the human connection between hideous evil loosed in the world. These hideous creatures are depicted as giant locusts (locusts were frequently used as a symbol of hard times or invading armies; cf. Joel 1:4-7; 2:1-9) who are given power for five months. Five is not an apocalyptic number, but people who resided in lands where the locust plagues could and did come, knew that the time for the locusts to appear was limited to a five-month "window" in the spring and summer.

The teaching is clear. The persecution inflicted on the people of God comes ultimately from the spiritual powers of evil, but the time allowed for such activity is not unlimited. There will be an end to periods of persecution. During that period God's people will survive. But not only will they suffer, others will be involved in the suffering also. The powers of evil show no favoritism in inflicting evil on the people of the world.

One of the interesting items in this scene is the detailed description of the locusts (vv. 7-10). The modern interpreter must be careful not to read this description so as to make the writer into a predictor of today's war machines. These were unknown to John, and the apocalyptic symbolism is so typical that one knows not to impose such interpretations on the text. Interesting particularly is that these hideous creatures have human faces. Evil has no entrance into the world except through human agency. Their spiritual leader is called Apollyon, the "Destroyer," an apt designation.

9:13-21: The sixth trumpet continues to describe a judgment that affects the earth. It is still a partial judgment but nonetheless a horrible scene.

The primary point of this section seems to be at the conclusion (vv. 20-21). The question could well be asked, Why is God's final judgment delayed? Why is the judgment only partial? The answer is clear: God is giving even the persecutors an opportunity to repent, but while that is true, the persecution on God's people continues.

79

The seventh trumpet has yet to be blown. Perhaps that will indicate the "end" of this evil persecution. Before the author describes that last trumpet, there is another interlude. The symmetry between the two cycles to this point is remarkably similar. Remarkable also is the similarity in the basic teaching of the cycles. Evil is self-destructive, but God also is involved in the judgment. The people of God suffer, but God will not allow them to be ultimately or finally defeated. Their witness is important to the final triumph of God's will.

An Interlude (10:1–11:14)

10:1-7: This interlude begins with the description of an angel coming to earth whose characteristics specifically link the being with the vision of God in chapter 4 and the vision of the Son of man in chapter 1. Clearly, he is the representative of these beings. The purpose of the angel seems to be to announce the "seven thunders," but the command is given to "seal up what the seven thunders have said, and do not write it down" (v. 4). The specific identification of the seven thunders and the reason why they could not be written down are, naturally, highly debated.

The best conjecture of what these thunders were seems to be another cycle of judgment. All the numbered cycles in this book are cycles of judgment, and there is no reason to doubt that these thunders, if enumerated, would have been essentially the same as the seven seals and the seven trumpets. It is not so obvious, but it is equally clear why they are not recorded. In apocalyptic there is almost always found the teaching that God shortens the time of suffering for the sake of the elect (cf. Mark 13:20). Describing another cycle of judgment would have indicated a longer period before the end of the persecution. If the cycle of the thunders is not written, then they will not come to pass, thus shortening the period of evil.

This understanding seems to be supported by the announcement in verse 6 that there will be "no more delay." The kjv has translated this "time no longer," which some have understood as the end of time, but the Greek idiom here is very specific and means what the rsv has rendered.

10:8-11: The seer is now commanded to take a scroll from the angel who has announced "no more delay." The scene is reminiscent of that in the book of Ezekiel where the prophet was also called on to "eat a scroll" (cf. Ezek. 2:8–3:3). The scroll is sweet to the mouth (it is always pleasing to denounce evil) but bitter to the stomach (the reality of judgment is never pretty no matter how well deserved).

11:1-14: The second part of the interlude contains some fascinating figures. (Some of the interpretations have also been rather fascinating.) The reader or hearer first learns that the temple of God was about to be measured. Measuring a place in biblical literature frequently connotes preservation or protection of what was measured. The temple is the place where God's people are to be gathered and thus protected so as to be able to survive the persecutions directed at them. The figure here obviously describes an especially harsh persecution since the "court outside the temple" (normally considered part of the temple but reserved for "observers") was not to be measured, in other words, protected. In periods of extreme persecution, there are no "gray" areas (such as the outer court would allow for). One must either choose to be one of God's people or choose to be the enemy of that people. In apocalyptic times there are only two sides—no others.

How long are these difficult periods to last? In typical apocalyptic fashion the answer comes: "forty-two months" (three and one half years). This number is not to be understood in a literal sense but rather in a figurative way—a short, indefinite period of time that will soon come to an end. During these days (1,260, also 3 1/2 years), two witnesses are given power to prophesy. Who are these witnesses?

Through all the centuries in which the church has struggled with the interpretation of Revelation, there are perhaps no figures that have been given more diverse identifications than these two witnesses. There are more than ten legitimate possibilities (and numerous others not at all in line with the meaning of the text). The most popular identification is to see these two as Enoch and Elijah, because according to some understandings of the biblical materials these two did not die a physical death. Since all humans must do that, the reasoning goes, these must be the two. Such an understanding is based on presuppositions brought to the text, however, rather than on what the text actually says.

According to John these two witnesses are generally described in the language of Zechariah 3–4, but they are even more specifically identified. One has the power to cause rain not to fall and to call fire down upon his enemies. The other has the power to unleash plagues on the earth. It does not take long for that designation to become clear—these two witnesses are Elijah and Moses (cf. I Kings 17–19; II Kings 1:9-12; Exodus 7–12). Why are these two singled out and what is the meaning in this context? To understand this figure, a bit of background is necessary. On numerous occasions in Hebrew thought, the person who was the first of a movement or the one who gave the movement identity and momentum was honored by having his name attached to the movement at large. For example, because Moses was the first great lawgiver of the Hebrew people, all laws go back to Moses. Thus Moses embodies the law. Likewise, Elijah was the first of the great individual prophets and was considered to be the embodiment of the prophetic movement.

Therefore, if someone wanted to allude to the law or the prophets, that person could simply say "Moses" or "Elijah." At this period of Jewish history, two of the three segments of the Hebrew scriptures had been accepted as canonical (authoritative) by the community. There were the *Torah* or Law and the *Nebi'im* or Prophets. Naturally they were frequently identified by Moses and Elijah, respectively. One sees this connection in other parts of the New Testament. For example, in the transfiguration story (Mark 9:2-8 and parallels), two figures appeared with Jesus at this place, and they were Moses and Elijah. This was to specify that Jesus was the fulfillment of the Law and the Prophets, the entire revelation of God as accepted and understood at that time.

In this context in Revelation, the text seems to be making the same identification with Moses and Elijah. Here, however, the Law and the Prophets are the responsibility of the people of God, that same group which was being persecuted by the powers of evil. The teaching here is a challenge to the church to continue witnessing to God's revelation and to preserve that revelation in the midst of these dark times. The representative of those evil forces (the beast) will make war on the people who hold to and espouse God's revelation, and God's people will indeed suffer and die for their witness. The persecution will last for a period designated by the number three and one half (surprise!).

There is much discussion about the identification of the "great city" (v. 8). That term is used on eight occasions in the book of Revelation, and in every other instance the explanation or clear intent is to identify the city as Rome. In this instance there are certain descriptions that some interpreters feel point to Jerusalem. After all that was where Jesus was crucified. The geography is not so important as the identification of the persecutors, however. It was the Roman government that executed Jesus; therefore, Rome is the better identification even here for the "great city."

The attempt to suppress and eradicate the "two witnesses" seems to have been a success. The joy of the enemy is short-lived, however, since the two are not only given new life but given God's approval by being exalted to heaven. Because of the faithfulness of the witnesses and their ultimate vindication by God, some people, but not all, give glory to God. The persecutors are judged, however. The martyr witness of the church with its faithfulness to God's revelation ultimately emerges victorious and produces positive results.

The reader is told in verse 14 that the second woe has been completed and the third will come quickly. There is a great deal of debate about the exact identity of the "three woes." The author is not so precise as the reader would like him to be in order to be able to identify positively these three items. It seems reasonable to assume that each "woe" represents one of the three cycles of judgment. The seven trumpets is the second and the seven bowls (cf. chs.

15–16) will be the last. Not all commentators agree on this, but it seems to make the best sense in the context of Revelation.

11:15-19: The reader or hearer is now introduced to the seventh trumpet. When it sounded the announcement came, "The kingdom of the world has become the kingdom of our Lord and of his Christ, and he shall reign for ever and ever." This is a very definitive statement. One sees no reason why everything should not now be concluded, that is, if one could decide such matters by twentieth-century logic and literary style. Yet such reasoning has been used and has led to numerous theories. One holds that chapters 4–11 were originally a separate, self-contained apocalypse, which John used and combined with other sources to form the book of Revelation as it now stands. This is certainly possible, but it is unnecessary to argue from that perspective. If one recalls that apocalyptic works are composed of a series of self-contained visionary units, each of which carries its own message and emphases, there is no real need to be upset over apparent chronological problems or to seek other sources (though it is quite possible that apocalyptic writers, including John, used such sources).

This cycle of the trumpets demonstrates God's active participation in judgment, describes the hideousness of the evil persecutors, tells the reader that God will shorten the time of persecution, calls for continued witness by the church to God's revelation, and concludes with a great statement of trust and praise to the effect that the victory is certain. The world's kingdom is already ruled over by God and Christ even though the final battles have not as yet been fought.

Part VI: A Historical Survey (Chapters 12–14)

One of the characteristics of apocalyptic literature is that in most apocalyptic works there is at least one section (if not more) where the author describes the flow of history from an earlier time to the current period of persecution. This serves to show how the present evil time has evolved. All of this is done in highly symbolic language, and the scene closes with a symbolic look into the future when the persecutor is destroyed and the people of God are secured from the judgment processes aimed at the instruments of evil (cf., e.g., Daniel 8). There are two of these scenes in Revelation, chapters 12–14 and chapters 17–19.

Many commentators have attempted to find in Revelation a series of episodes or scenes, each of which can be divided into seven parts. Such an approach is understandable in light of the fact that seven is such an important apocalyptic number and also because there are in Revelation itself three scenes that are specifically divided into seven sections. One must be careful, however, not to impose on the material patterns the author does not seem to imply either explicitly or implicitly. John usually makes clear those points where numbers or numbered scenes are to be understood by the reader or hearer. This episode (chs. 12–14) does not appear to lend itself to being divided into separate compartments. It is, rather, a typical "historical survey" depicting the background, present setting, and ultimate outcome of the difficulties being experienced by God's people at the hands of demonic evil and its earthly representatives.

12:1-6: The author begins the historical survey by depicting a woman surrounded by various apocalyptic symbols. Scholars have argued over the exact identification of the symbols related to the woman, but those issues are less important than the identity of the woman. On this point there is greater agreement. She clearly represents the people of God (cf. the twelve stars in the crown) She is pregnant and from her is to emerge a great leader, one who is to rule the nations, an obvious reference to the expected Messiah.

There also appears a great red dragon, a symbol of cosmic demonic evil, whose intent is to destroy the child the woman is to bear. John does not detail the events of Jesus' life—he expects that the readers and hearers will know about those matters. He simply states that in spite of all that the dragon can do, this one, born of the people of God, has been victorious and exalted to God's side. The dragon then turns on the woman (now representative of the new people of God), but she is protected in the wilderness (a place of evil and danger as well as a place of refuge) for 1,260 days (3 1/2 years), the length of time persecution is allowed to continue.

12:7-17: This scene answers the overall question, from both a broad and a narrow view, of why there is persecution directed against the church. The "war" is a continuing reality, the struggle between God and Satan, but the outcome has already been decided. God is the victor; Satan is the vanquished. Even though evil has been defeated at the highest echelons, the struggle still continues on earth. Those here are called on to participate by remaining faithful. By allying themselves with the victors in the struggle they can participate in the rewards accompanying victory.

The anger and wrath of the powers of evil are directed at the woman and her offspring (v. 13). She is given the wings of the eagle to fly into the wilderness.

Both of these are figures drawn from the Exodus event to enhance the point of God's protection and guidance for God's people. Naturally the extent of this protection is three and one half, the length of the persecution.

Scholars have differed in their interpretations of verses 15-16. Do the figures of the water and flood, and the earth opening to swallow that river, have any definite symbolic significance, or are they general symbols simply given as part of the larger scene to add to the drama of the setting? Some have seen in this another reference to Exodus imagery (the episode at the Red Sea), while others think of this as rooted in the idea of the waters of primeval chaos, which threaten to undo God's creation. Still others have argued that the figure refers to the catacombs of Rome where Christians could at times take refuge in periods of persecution. No general agreement can be found, and probably the best way to understand the symbolism here is in a general way. God controls all things in such a way as to ensure the safety of the woman and her offspring. This does not, however, mean that there is no danger. Any who are faithful and loyal can expect the opposition of Satan's cohorts.

The section ends with Satan (the dragon) standing on the sand of the sea. In apocalyptic, evil empires usually arise from the sea, one of the great sources of evil (cf. Daniel 7). Here the dragon is about to summon and enlist assistance for his onslaught against the people of God.

13:1-4: At this point there appears from the sea a hideous beast, which very much resembles the dragon itself. Further, the beast is described as a combination of the beasts of Daniel 7. This beast, a human government, has been given the power of the dragon. It also has seven heads (a reference to rulers), but one of these has a "mortal wound," which has been healed. This figure has caused interpreters some problems, but the solution to the identity of the "wounded head" should be reserved until the entire section has been examined. We shall return to this problem.

The primary focus of the teaching here is the emphasis on the transfer of power to the beast by the dragon and the subsequent awe in which the people of the world hold the beast. They worship it; but in reality they are worshiping the dragon. Evil exercises its authority over people by deception. The reader notes that the beast has not as yet been specifically identified. All one knows at this point is that it is a nation.

13:5-10: The beast is now described more fully. It is an agent of evil, and it blasphemes God. God's people are subjected to a cruel "war," and they are "conquered." Of course this situation lasts for forty-two months (three and one half years), the apocalyptic period during which evil runs amok. For the people to whom this book was originally addressed, there would have been no mystery at all about the identity of this beast. It was the Roman state, which was directing its power against them. The call is for "endurance" on the part of these persecuted people.

One final issue in this section stems from the reference to the "book of life." This is a figure found in apocalyptic writings that served as a symbol of additional support and hope for the persecuted people. If a name was recorded in a book, especially a book associated with God, that gave the person whose name was listed a degree of security. The "name," that is, the person, could not be removed by anyone or anything. No matter the sacrifice, not even death could remove one's name from the book. The only threat to having one's name erased lay in one's own response to the persecution. If one remained loyal, one's place in God's kingdom was certain; but if one became apostate, one gave up one's right to a place "in the book." The ultimate outcome rested strictly on the person's action in the face of the forces of evil.

13:11-18: This section has been a focal point in the history of the interpretation of Revelation. Many theories have been presented identifying the "lamb-beast" and the mysterious number "666." If the reader will remain consistent in understanding the passage in an apocalyptic manner, the "mysteries" become much clearer.

The figure of the lamb-beast is one of John's antithetical symbols (defined as two symbols that outwardly look alike but that are exactly opposite from each other). The reader has already encountered the Lamb of chapter 5, the agent of God, a religious figure. Here, this lamb is also a religious figure, but it speaks "like a dragon." This lamb represents the official priesthood, which was established to ensure that people worship the beast (a nation) that was allied with the dragon, Satan. The descriptions given in verses 13-15 are very similar to the deceptive practices carried out and cultic apparatuses used by religious officials in many of the different temples of the Graeco-Roman world. Ignorant and superstitious people could be manipulated by idols that moved or talked, and archaeologists have discovered ancient temples where wires and pulleys were used to mesmerize the unsuspecting and gullible.

The most important aspect of this lamb-beast is that it has the power to allow or disallow the people's participation in the continuing life of the community, especially participation in the economic marketplace (v. 17). Those who worship the beast receive a "mark." Many have wondered about this mysterious badge. There is no real mystery, however, since in those days slaves were frequently branded on the hand or forehead to distinguish clearly whose property they were. The mark then is the clear designation that these people belonged to the beast. Whether John had in mind here a literal mark or used that idea symbolically could be debated. In either instance, however, the meaning is the same. Unless one cooperated with the beast and its cohorts, a person could not "buy or sell," an effective way of mandating compliance with the state.

Throughout the history of the church, there have been few matters that have raised as much controversy as the identification of the number 666. Many different identifications have been given: the Muslim Empire at the time of the Crusades, the Muslim leader Saladin, the Pope, Martin Luther, Napoleon, Kaiser Wilhelm, Hitler, Tojo, Mussolini, Stalin, North Korea, North Vietnam, Henry Kissinger, the European Common Market, a giant computer in Belgium, and so on. The mark of the beast has been identified as a literal 666 branded on the forehead of people, social security numbers, the universal product code (Bar Code) on packages, and so forth. These identifications have been made by honest and sincere people throughout church history. Each identification has turned out to be wrong (at least in the way the identification was made). The reason is simple: This passage is not predicting something or someone to come in the future, but rather is describing something that the people of that time and place were experiencing and would recognize.

One also notes something curious about this text.

There is no mention of an "antichrist." This term has been used so frequently of figures in the New Testament, and especially of the beast here in Revelation 13, that almost everyone refers to this figure by that term. The author of Revelation, however, does not. In fact John never uses the term once in the entire book! The only places where the term does appear in the New Testament are in the Johannine letters where the antichrist is defined as one who denies that Jesus has come in the flesh (cf. I John 2:22). Since John does not use the term in Revelation and since so many people today already have some definitions present in their thinking about "the antichrist," it seems best not to use that designation for this or other figures in Revelation. The best approach is to allow John to define and describe these figures as he wishes.

The beast is finally about ready to be identified, but the author gives a cryptic designation, a number. There was no system of arabic numerals then; therefore, in those days most peoples counted by letters of their alphabets. Since letters carried numerical value, every person had both a name and a number. One recalls the writing on the wall of a house in Pompeii: "I love her whose number is 545." (This system of names and numbers is called *gematria*.) When John says that the beast's number is "a human number," he means that it is a man's name. The name totals 666, though in some ancient Greek manuscripts and versions the number is 616.

It seems clear that the identity of this name is to be connected with the wounded head on the beast that has come back to life. Heads on beasts represent rulers in apocalyptic, so this head is obviously a Roman ruler. The Hebrews (and later, Christians too) had a tendency to concretize entire movements

in the first person who began or gave impeti
movement (cf. part V, pp. 82-83).

The question here centers on the persecution of
Christians. What Roman ruler was the first to
persecute the Christians? The answer is Nero, who
used the Christians in Rome as scapegoats for the fire
he had set in Rome in the mid sixties. When the fire
proved to be a political liability for Nero, he looked at
the new religious group in town and blamed them.
Some were crucified, some beheaded, some were
dressed in animal skins and wild dogs were turned
loose on them, some dipped in tar, tied in trees, and
used as human torches to serve as lighting for Nero's
famous garden parties. This information comes to us
not from the Christians directly but from Roman
writers! Since Nero had been the first Roman
emperor to persecute the Christians, any subsequent
Roman ruler who also did that would be known as
"Nero," or perhaps "Nero reborn." (It is interesting
that even some of the Romans and other people of the
world of that time believed that Nero would return!)
Domitian, the present ruler who was persecuting the
Christians, would have been understood by them to
be the reincarnation of Nero.

How does this identification of Domitian with Nero
assist the interpreter with the number 666 or 616? It
seems logical that, whatever solution is reached, the
two numbers must both be a part of the solution. One
finds that if the name and title "Nero Caesar" is
placed into Aramaic (Hebrew) characters and the
numerical designations for those letters are totaled,
there is a solution to the problem. One can spell the
name Nero either Nero or Neron. Thus if one spells
the name and title with the extra n, the total is 666. If
the name and title are used without the extra n the
total is 616. To illustrate:

Neron Caesar = 666 = נרון קסר
Nero Caesar = 616 = נרו קסר

In Hebrew (Aramaic), the letters used here hold the following numerical values:

נ nun = 50		ק qoph = 100
ר resh = 200		ס samech = 60
ו waw = 6		ן (final) nun = 50

One can see that the total of the numbers of the one is 666, and the total of the other is 616. It must readily be admitted that there is no absolute consensus among scholars that this solution is the correct one to this text. Other possibilities have been proposed such as the emperor Vespasian, or Titus, or the Roman Empire itself (the Greek numbering of *Lateinos*, i.e., Latin, Latin empire, being 666). None of these identifications, however, solves the 616 problem, and John tells the reader that this is a man's name, not a designation for an empire.

Some have even argued that the number six has a special meaning, designating complete imperfection since it comes so close to seven but falls one short. This interpretation seems to be rather fanciful and a *later* understanding read back into the author's time. Six is simply not an apocalyptic number. The most likely and logical conclusion is that the wounded head figure and the 666 (616) gematria are best explained as references to Nero. Since Nero was the first Roman emperor to persecute the Christians, any later emperor who did so could easily be depicted as Nero reborn. This identification fits the historical context, was understandable to the people for whom it was written, seems to be the most likely interpretation of the passage, and was considered the correct identification early in Christian interpretation of this text.

14:1-5: The survey shifts now to describe those who are not followers of the beast; these belong to the Lamb and bear its name written on their foreheads in contrast to those who bear the mark of the beast. These "marks" denote to whom these people belong and have pledged their allegiance. The number of those who belong to the Lamb is 144,000, again a multiple of ten and twelve denoting "all" the people of God.

The primary characteristic of these people seems on first reading peculiar. One reads, they "have not defiled themselves with women, for they are [virgins]." If one is to be a literalist, these people must be all male and never have had sexual relations. The term in the Greek is inclusive regarding gender, however, and one recalls that in much of the biblical literature unfaithfulness to God and apostasy are often described figuratively under the image of sexual impurity or harlotry. It is clear that this is the connotation here. Those who learn this "new song" are those who have remained faithful and loyal and have not gone over to the side of the "beast" during the period of persecution. They have not been "seduced" by that deception.

14:6-13: Now the "look ahead" is announced with this assurance that those who worship the beast will share in the fate of the beast. That fate is to be determined by God, and it will not be a pretty sight!

In verse 8 the reader is introduced to a designation of the persecutor that has not occurred before in this book but will appear again. The announcement is that "Babylon the great" will fall. From the context it is clear that the term refers to the beast. It is also

clear from chapter 13 that the beast is Rome. How did
this identification come to be made? Why is Babylon
an appropriate designation for Rome?

One recalls once more the tendency of the Jewish
and (later) Christian communities to concretize
movements in the first significant person or entity in
the series or cycle. The first nation to capture
Jerusalem (after David) and destroy the Temple was
Babylonia (586 B.C.). When Rome captured Jerusalem
and sacked and burned the city and destroyed (or
partially destroyed) the Temple in A.D. 70, the Jewish
(and Christian) communities began to refer to Rome
as Babylon. Since this was a widely known figure, the
author of Revelation used it in his work.

The announcement of the wrath of God to be visited
on all who ally themselves with the beast is graphic
indeed: "He also shall drink the wine of God's wrath
[a vehement fury], poured unmixed into the cup of
[God's] anger" (v. 10a). There is another call for the
endurance of the saints (v. 12) because one does not
wish to falter now with the end of the persecution in
sight. There is, further, a solemn promise that those
who lay down their lives in the cause of the Lord will
receive a special reward. Their "deeds" will not be
forgotten.

14:14-20: The reader or hearer now comes to the
conclusion of the historical survey. This segment
describes the judgment on the persecutor. The scene
here is depicted as a harvest. The "harvester" comes
on the cloud (a typical apocalyptic designation for the
one who executes God's penalty on unbounded evil)
and begins the reaping by dividing the good grain
from the weeds, from the unproductive grain or fruit,
and so on. The good harvest is protected; the rest is
destroyed. There are few people who have not at least

heard of this famous figure. God's judgment is symbolized as a great winepress, which is "trodden" outside the city. (The city is the place reserved for the good harvest. John will use this figure more fully later.) The red juice of the grapes signifies the blood of those who are to feel God's wrath, and this will constitute a veritable sea of blood as high as a "horse's bridle" for "one thousand six hundred stadia" (v. 20).

There are those, naturally, who calculate how far 1,600 stadia would reach. The answer is about 200 miles, and some speculate where such a large geographical area would be. To do this, however, is to miss the point of the apocalyptic symbolism. The number 1,600 is a multiple of the number 4 (representing the created order, the earth here) and 10 (indicating inclusiveness). God's judgment reaches anywhere in this world where that judgment is deserved. Here it is primarily centered on the beast and its followers.

Part VII: The Final Cycle of Judgment
(Chapters 15–16)

At this point the author presents the last of the three cycles (the numbered cycles) of judgment. In the previous cycles the judgment was partial, but now the good news is proclaimed that with these episodes the "wrath of God is ended" (15:1). The word translated "ended" is in Greek the word that indicates that something has come to fulfillment, completion, maturity. It is not "ended" in the sense of a final, last, chronological judgment but "ended" in that the persecution has now come to its moment of completion.

15:1-4: Chapter 15 basically serves as an introduction to the seven bowls of chapter 16. The verses here (1-4) announce that the judgment on the persecutor has come to the moment of completion. The seer is shown the "sea of glass" (cf. ch. 4), this time "mingled with fire." The tranquility of the scene where God's throne stood is now charged with the fire of God's judgment. Participating in the judgment are those who have "conquered the beast and its image and the number of its name." The witness of those who have remained faithful and loyal even to death is an intimate component in the judgment of the forces of evil. The seemingly conquered ones are the real victors in this struggle. Their witness is not in vain but will be rewarded, and their witness will have influence and power beyond their time and place.

15:5-8: These verses dramatically depict the final prelude to the judgment of the bowls, which is about to come. The reader or hearer is again reminded that the sure hope for the truth of this scenario is directly related to the scene in chapter 4. Figures from that account appear here also. This is a solemn scene, worthy of the significance of the occasion. The reference to no one's being able to enter the temple probably signifies that it is now too late for those who have been afforded the time and opportunity to repent to do so, having delayed because of the circumstances of the times. God's mercy is all encompassing, but there is a limit to divine patience. There are "points of no return" even in religious and spiritual relationships.

16:1-9: One cannot but recognize the similarity of images in this cycle with the cycle of the seven trumpets. The Exodus figures are quite prominent here as there. Each of the scenes contributes to the overall portrait of judgment. Perhaps two items should be cited as especially significant in this section.

There is, first of all, the idea that the penalty for a curse or sin should be appropriate to the act. This was certainly true in Old Testament teachings and is continued in the New Testament writings as well. Here in Revelation the same principle holds:

> For men have shed the blood of saints and prophets,
> and thou hast given them blood to drink.
> It is their due!
>
> (v. 6)

The second point to be especially noted is the reference at the conclusion of verse 9. In spite of all the judgments and in spite of knowing that these had come from God because of their activity and participation in demonic evil, people still did not begin to repent and give glory to God. This is reminiscent of the great saying of Satan in Milton's *Paradise Lost*, "Better to reign in hell than serve in heav'n" (book I, line 262). There are those who, given the right of option, will reject God beyond the point of no return.

16:10-16: The reader or hearer learns here specifically that these judgments are directed at the beast and those who follow the beast. This is clear in the episode of the fifth bowl (vv. 10-11).

One of the most controversial passages in the book of Revelation is now encountered. An invasion from the east is described, a gathering for a great battle at the place called Armageddon. Far too much has usually been read into this passage, and it is necessary to examine the passage to see what it does and does not teach.

The figure of the invaders from the east is an apocalyptic means to raise the specter of the judgment on Rome. The Parthian Empire, great successor to the old Persian Empire, was greatly feared in that section of the world by the Romans. To suggest this figure was a means John used to bolster the hopes of the faithful. God could and would use others to break the yoke of Rome's persecution. It was typical in apocalyptic writings to attempt to identify how the persecutor was to be destroyed. The major point with the apocalyptic writer was not whether the actual speculation came to pass exactly but whether the result, the removal of the persecutor, was accomplished. (One is reminded of the scenario painted in Daniel 11:40-45 where specific details given by the apocalyptic writer did not materialize exactly, but the major issue came to pass—the persecution was ended and the proscription against Judaism was lifted.)

An assembling for battle is now described (v. 14). This gathering takes place at Armageddon. Who has not heard of this awesome place and of the horrors associated with the great conflict there? In attempting to understand this passage correctly the interpreter must be careful to understand the apocalyptic background and not to read into the text ideas that have been popularly espoused about this scene.

Perhaps the greatest mystery to most persons about Armageddon lies in understanding what this mysterious place is. The interpreter notes first that the word *Armageddon* is not a Greek word but is borrowed from Hebrew or Aramaic. (Reference has already been given to the strong Semitic background for this book.) Numerous identifications of the word have been made. To cite only a few, one finds "marauding mountain," "the desirable city," "the fruitful mountain," "the mountain of meeting,"

among others. Some have made specific identifications based on geography: "Mt. Carmel," "the city of
Megiddo," or "the mount (hill) of Megiddo." One can
find linguistic or geographic support for any of these
identifications. Most commentators, however, think
that the term derives from the Hebrew city Megiddo.
(Whether the "Ar" or "Har" with it refers to "city" or
"mountain" is largely irrelevant.)

Why would that city be of some significance in this
context? One recalls that in the history of ancient
Israel (and Judah) many of the most significant
battles that had great influence for the people of God
were fought at or near Megiddo. The reason for this
lay in the geographical setting of the city. It was near
the entryway into the land from the north in the
plain of Esdraelon or Valley of Jezreel and was
strategically located at the place where invaders
were best confronted so as to keep them out of the
land. Good and bad things had happened for the
people of God at or near Megiddo (cf. Judges 4–5; I
Kings 9:15; II Kings 23:29), and the city was
mentioned in texts from other nations of the ancient
world (especially Egyptian). It was a place for
significant battles.

The interesting aspect of the description of
Armageddon in this bowl cycle is that no battle is
fought. They gather for battle, but God intervenes (in
typical apocalyptic fashion) and destroys the enemies
of the people of God without a battle. One also notes
with interest that this is the *only* place in the entire
Bible where the term *Armageddon* is found. It is not
even mentioned again in Revelation, much to the
surprise of many. Some still talk about a great battle
to be fought at Armageddon, and others presently
even interpret this reference as a description of an

entire war fought over a long period of time. Neither
of these ideas can be found in the text, however.

16:17-20: The seventh bowl describes in typical
apocalyptic imagery the fall of "Babylon." By now
everyone knows that Babylon represents Rome, the
persecutor of God's people. One notes here that there
is no battle. God intervenes directly and judges the
"great city." In verse 20 there are references to
islands and mountains (hills). Some commentators
understand the islands to be a reference to the
Roman islands used for detaining banished people
(such as John, perhaps?) and the hills to be a
reference to the hills upon which Rome had been
built. The scene is one of desperation, but it depicts
judgment on the persecutors. Interestingly enough
those who are judged still blame God for their fate—a
fate they have *chosen.*

Part VIII: A Historical Survey (Chapters 17-19)

Once again John describes the situation in which
the persecuted find themselves, depicting the persecutor and the destruction of the persecutor (cf. chs.
12-14). The major emphasis in this section resides in
the fall of "Babylon" and the description of that fall.

17:1-6: The seer is now told that he is about to
witness the judgment of the "great harlot." The
reader or hearer at this point does not know precisely
who or what this great harlot is. After all that John
has described before, however, one would be surprised if it were not another description of the
persecutor, Rome.

John relates that he saw a woman seated upon a
"scarlet beast." One notes with interest that the
description of this beast is quite like that of the beast

of chapter 13. The woman is obviously representative of some form of authority and power. Her name, "Babylon the great," was written on her forehead. Some scholars argue that the name on the forehead is appropriate because harlots in Rome wore labels above their eyes with their names on them. Others dispute this, however. The relevant point is that the name signifies something about the being described (cf. 13:16; 14:1). This woman represents the political system at that time persecuting God's people. She was "drunk with the blood of the saints and [even] the blood of the martyrs of Jesus" (v. 6).

Already in Revelation the term *Babylon* has been used and has been identified as symbolic of Rome. The ensuing explanation will now make that identification very clear.

17:7-14: At this point, again in typical apocalyptic fashion, the narrator viewing these images is puzzled. An angel, however, is on the scene to explain the grotesque images to the befuddled observer.

The beast is described as one who was, is not, and is to arise from the bottomless pit. This is, of course, the antithesis of John's favorite description for God, "The One who is, was, and is to come." The operational procedure of the beast is again deception (cf. 13:3-4), and all whose names are not written in the book (cf. part VI, pp. 89-90) will be misled. The explanation is then given. The seven heads on the beast represent "seven [hills] on which the woman is seated." It would not take anyone in that day longer than an instant to make the connection with the famous seven hills on which Rome was founded and built. Clearly, the woman is Rome (Babylon). John could not have been much more explicit if he had drawn a picture and labeled it with huge letters.

The author, however, uses the seven heads in

another way. He says that the seven heads represent seven rulers. This identification has caused a great amount of debate among scholars. Some argue that this figure must be understood in concrete historical terms, and they attempt to identify precisely the emperor being described. No real unanimity can be found since few can agree on where to begin the countdown for the emperors. Does one begin with Julius or Augustus Caesar? Does one count the "year of the three emperors" (i.e., A.D. 68–69, a short period of political instability when Rome had three emperors in rapid succession), or count the three as one, or ignore all of them since no one could really gain substantial control? The debate is sometimes rather hotly contested because understanding the precise identity of the emperor could help in dating the book (or at least this passage). For example, if one began the count with Julius, the sixth emperor is Nero. If one begins with Augustus, and omits the three, the eighth is Domitian. If one begins with Nero, and counts the three, the seventh is Domitian, and so on.

If interpreters really expect to find some genuine historical detail here, they will probably be disappointed and frustrated. There are simply too many variables. If, however, one recalls that this is apocalyptic symbolism, the meaning of this explanation becomes more certain. Seven is the number that denotes something having come to maturity or fruition. The description of the seven as rulers, "five of whom have fallen," (i.e., are already past), "one is, the other has not yet come, and when he comes he must remain only a little while" (v. 10), clearly teaches that the end of the persecution is near but still has a short period of time to run its course. The specific identification of the emperor in this passage is really a modern concern and not of great importance.

The identification of the beast, however, is another matter. John clearly wants the readers to be able to identify this figure. It is an "eighth," which belongs "to the seven"; that is, the demonic character of the beast (as it now is) is taken from one of the past rulers who has been "reborn" (figuratively, not literally). This obviously refers to Nero, the first emperor to persecute the Christian community. His evil is reborn in this persecution of the people of God by Domitian.

The "ten kings" has also caused some identification problems. They are described as "ten kings who have not yet received royal power" but who will for a short time, together with the beast (v. 12). Most likely they signify those who have allied themselves with the beast in its persecution of God's people. Whether John means to specify here any particular collaborators with Rome or whether he simply lumps such lackeys together as "ten kings" is debated. The important idea is that the powers and forces of evil recruit as many as they can to "make war on the Lamb." It is the classic apocalyptic struggle between good and evil, between God and those allied with God against the beast and those allied with it. The ultimate victory is already ensured; it has been won by the Lamb and those with him. The martyr witness of the church becomes a part of that victory.

17:15-18: The interpreter now encounters a puzzling account. The beast and the "ten horns" will hate the harlot, turn on her, and destroy her. One of the obvious intents of this is to teach that evil is self-destructive, but that does not really seem to be the most important idea John wants the reader or hearer to understand. John now seems to separate the beast from the harlot. In addition to the teaching that the evil powers cannot trust even their own allies, the passage seems to indicate that the harlot (in this specific context the one who is persecuting the saints of God, v. 6) can be separated from the beast (Rome) and that Rome as a nation will continue after the persecution (the harlot) is removed.

Finally, the author makes certain that the reader or hearer will understand exactly who this woman is (if the seven hills did not make it clear!). The woman is the "great city which has dominion over the kings of the earth" (v. 18). What city at that time fit that description? Rome, of course.

18:1-8: With the announcement that the harlot is to be destroyed there is now a funeral dirge delivered over the fall of the harlot city. There are some parallels between this passage and the funeral dirge of Amos over the nation of Israel (cf. Amos 5:1-3). The tense of the verbs is past, not because this is an announcement after the fact, but rather because John believes so strongly that this judgment will assuredly take place.

There is a call for the people of God to "come out of her." This also is a typical apocalyptic device that warns of the impending judgment on the persecutor. The good people are to get away so that they will not be caught in that judgment and suffer additional hardships (cf. Mark 13:14-18).

The poetic description here depicts the harlot as being burned. Some interpreters make much of this, relating that punishment to Old Testament penalties for some cases of incest or harlotry or failure to obey God's word (cf. Lev. 21:9). Perhaps, but the major point is that the fire represents God's judgment on this group, which has allied itself with demonic evil and which has persecuted the people of God.

18:9-20: Next follows a list of all those who will share in some way in this judgment. There are many who have connected themselves with the harlot for their own gain—kings of the earth, merchants, traders, any who profit by this association. All of these stand to lose because of the harlot's demise. It is interesting to note that all of these stand "far off" when the judgment comes, and though they are not directly judged, they are all affected.

The passage here depicts both the good that Rome had done and could bring about as well as the evil excesses, which caused it to go "over the brink." Certain activities of a political state were not viewed as inherently evil, but the excesses put the state's actions into the category of demonic evil. For example, the listing in verses 11-13 gives the clue. Traffic in items and merchandise is not evil, but when the traffic deals in "human lives" it has gone beyond legitimate bounds. For this, the judgment will come.

Verse 20 clearly teaches that the judgment is rendered on behalf of those who have remained faithful and loyal. It is for them that Babylon has been destroyed. The martyr witness of the saints is an essential ingredient in God's victory over the powers and forces of evil and the judgment on those forces.

18:21-24: These verses summarize the case against the harlot city, and the angel announces the results of that judgment.

19:1-8: The description now shifts back to the heavenly scene (cf. chs. 4–5) where there is celebration over the fall of Babylon and a reaffirmation that the judgment is just and a result of the faithfulness of the martyrs.

Depicted here is the marriage of the Lamb and the

107

Bride (i.e., the church), who is clothed in the finest of wedding splendor. This splendor is "the righteous deeds of the saints." The word translated "righteous deeds" signifies the "right" things that these people do because of their relationship with God and the Lamb. There is not here a doctrine of "works righteousness," however, as a few have argued.

19:9-10: The angel delivers a blessing on those who have been "invited" to the marriage supper of the Lamb. The emphasis here is not on "invited" so much as on those who have accepted the invitation. John falls down to worship the angel, but he is told sternly, "You must not do that!" This is a most appropriate scene. After all, the people of God are being asked (required) to worship the Roman state and its emperor. When John attempts to worship God's angel, he is told that this should not be done. The true believer can respect, admire, and appreciate all those who contribute positively to the world and its well-being, but worship is another matter. Only God is to be worshiped.

The last sentence has caused interpreters some problems. What do the "testimony of Jesus" and "the spirit of prophecy" mean? Is it Jesus' testimony that is at stake here or the testimony about Jesus? Either could be meant, but in the context of this book it seems that the better choice would be the believer's testimony to or about Jesus. That is the way believers have to demonstrate that their loyalty is to God and to God alone.

The other phrase, "the spirit of prophecy," is even more difficult to understand. Prophecy in the biblical writings is never primarily prediction of the future but rather the proclamation of God's word to the world (especially to God's people) at certain moments for certain purposes. In this instance the testimony of the martyr church *is* the proclamation of God's word to that time and moment of history (cf. 11:1-13). The "word" of God can be delivered in numerous ways. Witnessing to God's word in a time of persecution is one of the most powerful witnesses for that word in this world.

19:11-16: At this point John describes God's agent who is to be responsible for the funeral dirge over the great harlot. The reader cannot but recall other images from some of the other visionary scenes in Revelation. The rider sits on a white horse (cf. the other rider in 6:1-2), is described by some of the symbols of 1:12-16, has a name no one knows (cf. 2:17), rules with a rod of iron (cf. 12:5), and will tread the winepress of God's wrath (cf. 14:19-20). There is obvious parallelism here between the present visionary unit of chapters 17–19 and that of chapters 12–14, and numerous symbols and images are drawn from different components of the overall book.

One must be cautious not to "overinterpret" these images. The overall scene and its meaning are the most important items about which to be concerned. God's agent, who is to bring the end of the persecution, is described primarily as a victor (note the use of the color white). The author is not here attempting to describe *how* the judgment is to take place but rather *who* is responsible for it. The point is squarely put: God's agent, the Lamb, the Christ, is the One who wins the ultimate victory, not the conqueror who went out "conquering and for the sake of conquering" (6:2).

There are two primary interpretative points in this passage: Where does the "blood" originate? and why is the name inscribed on the "thigh"? There are several interpretations of each of these figures. The blood could have come from the people who are being judged, the persecutors, or it could be the blood of the martyrs, or it could be the blood of the rider. Some argue that the blood really denotes ritual sprinkling as in a sacrificial setting. Several theories could be correct, but the most plausible in this context seems to be one that is connected with the blood of sacrificial living dedicated to the service of God. This could be Jesus' own blood or the martyrs' blood or both. The most important element is that this blood has won the victory over evil and its cohorts.

The question about the name on the thigh has several answers also. Some argue that statues in that time sometimes had names carved on the thigh; others have argued that the Greeks sometimes branded their horses on the thigh; still others believe that the name is not really on the thigh but on the hem of the mantle that falls over the thigh or on the girdle worn by some in battle. One recent commentator has argued that an Aramaic source has been mistranslated. The word for "thigh" and the word for "banner" are so close that they have been confused. Thus the text should have read, "on his banner" (cf. J. M. Ford, *Revelation*, p. 323). The important aspect here is not where the inscription is so much as what the name is. That shows what the true character and essence of the rider are. The name is "King of kings and Lord of lords," that is, the greatest king, the greatest lord.

19:17-21: The final scene in this visionary unit is a highly symbolic description of the destruction of the persecutor. Far too many interpreters take this as a literal description of a literal event, but in apocalyptic the fall and demise of the persecutor are usually depicted in gory scenes of wholesale slaughter. Again the point is not how this is to happen but that the persecution is soon to be over. The destruction of those who have pressed the persecution is vividly described because that destruction involves not simply a physical removal from the scene but an ultimate delegation of those who have allied themselves with cosmic evil to a cosmic and eternal relationship with that evil. There is a special place for such wickedness and for those who have chosen to be a part of it—the lake of fire that burns with brimstone. This is, of course, a symbolic image and will be defined more specifically in the final visionary scene.

Part IX: The Final Vision (20:1–22:5)

Chapters 20:1–22:5 constitute the last of the visionary units of this marvelous apocalyptic work. Included in this portion is one of three sections of Revelation that are so frequently misunderstood and so horribly abused. The three passages are chapter 13, chapter 17, and chapter 20. Two of these have been examined already.

According to Darbyist schemes (and those influenced by Darbyism) the twentieth chapter should be understood as teaching something like this: Jesus returns; Jesus binds Satan; there is a thousand-year *earthly* reign of Jesus with a group of believers (exactly who these are is disputed); Satan is loosed; there is a final battle, which ends all of human history; there is a final judgment with all receiving their just reward—either eternity in heaven or eternity in hell. In some schemes there are many other components imported into the scene from other parts of the Scripture. The basic structure outlined above, however, is taken from chapter 20 of Revelation. The interpreter needs to put aside all that has formerly been understood as part of the scenario and allow John to describe the scene as he intended his readers and hearers to understand it.

One of the problems modern interpreters have in interpreting this passage (and others in Revelation also) lies in the area of chronology. Revelation has long been viewed as a chronological scheme with one episode or series of events following another in a linear sequence until the *end* comes. Most apocalyptic literature, however, concentrates less on linear chronology than on "states" or "episodes," that have meaning within themselves! The interpreter has already encountered in Revelation several examples of what could be the *end* if these passages were to be understood literally and chronologically. If the reader interprets these passages in that way, however, the whole book loses any semblance of meaning and order. If one does not understand the basic methodology of the apocalyptic writer, the material makes no sense whatsoever.

If this major point can be kept firmly in mind as the interpreter comes to the book of Revelation in general and chapters 20:1–22:5 in particular, the meaning will become clear. If one seeks to find in this passage a specific chronology, confusion will reign. Many interpreters do indeed miss this important consideration when approaching this text, and there have been numerous attempts to rearrange the text so as to force the material into a logical chronology. In apocalyptic writings that is not necessary and does real damage to the intended meaning of the text.

20:1-3: The entire section is introduced with a description of an angel coming down from heaven. One notes immediately that this is *not* Jesus. It is an angel, a servant of God and Christ. This servant seizes Satan and binds him "for a thousand years." The interpreter by now knows immediately that the number 1,000 is not intended to be understood literally. This figure being a multiple of ten indicates completeness or inclusiveness. Satan's being bound for a thousand years means simply that Satan is completely bound. This binding is accomplished by one of God's servants. What could this mean?

The most likely explanation in the midst of the context of Revelation is that John believes that the total commitment of God's servants is the means by which Satan is bound in this world. His plea to the Christians under persecution is to keep the faith. By so doing they have a part in the destruction that ultimately will come upon the powers of evil, and they are even now limiting the influence of Satan in the world.

The primary problem in this passage (as in v. 7 below) concerns the clause "Till the thousand years were ended." (In v. 7 the RSV reads, "And when the thousand years are ended.") In the English translations this text reads as if it were an indicative statement, in other words that it is true and straightforward as stated. In the Greek text, however, the verb is in the subjunctive mood (as it is in v. 7). The subjunctive mood in Greek, as in English, denotes doubt, hesitancy, or contingency; thus, the idea of the ending of the thousand years has some sort of doubt or contingency to it. What causes this? It appears from the text that the hesitancy is to be linked with the faithfulness of the persecuted. One recalls that it is the angel or servant of God who binds Satan.

20:4-6: In this segment John describes those "for whom judgment was given." The RSV translation "to whom judgment was committed" is misleading and not as accurate a rendering of the Greek text. Judgment is given for those who have been faithful. These are described here as the martyrs. (The reference to "beheading" is probably singled out since that was the specific Roman form of punishment for citizens.) Their great virtue is the fact that they did not worship the beast.

Perhaps the primary interpretative problem with this section lies in where these martyrs live and reign with Christ for a thousand years. For many years this passage was interpreted as Christ with the church in the world until the *end* came. In short, this millennial kingdom is the church present in the world until the time when Jesus returns to complete the work begun in his lifetime. (This view is popularly known as postmillennialism since Jesus is to return *after* the thousand-year reign; cf. above, pp. 30-31.)

When the Darbyist system began to become widespread and influential, the advocates of that position taught that the millennial reign of Jesus with the saints had not yet taken place. That eventuality would come after Jesus returned to establish the kingdom. Thus the emphasis in this scheme was known as premillennialism since Jesus was to return before the thousand-year reign. Many persons who are not themselves pure Darbyists nevertheless hold to this particular viewpoint.

The interesting point in these theories is that both assume that the thousand-year kingdom is (1) a rather literal thousand-year period, and (2) on this earth. The question is whether either of these assumptions is correct. If one examines the text, it is clear that the number 1,000 has been used in Revelation up to this chapter in a truly apocalyptic manner. A thousand is a multiple of ten, the number signifying inclusiveness, completeness, or totality. Why would John suddenly use the term literally? And in this obviously apocalyptic setting, when it could be misunderstood so easily? The answer is that John uses the term here as he has throughout the book—in a symbolic manner to denote completeness, inclusiveness, and totality. The saints who give their lives for the cause of God and Christ win a victory that assures them of a special relationship with Christ totally and completely. This is John's description of the special reward for the martyrs, something found in almost every apocalyptic work.

Further, where are these people reigning? As noted previously the premillennialists and postmillennialists argue that the earth is the place of this scenario. If one examines the text carefully, however, it becomes rather obvious that John is not talking about the earth but is describing a scene in *heaven*. The martyrs are in heaven here and in every other place in Revelation (cf. 6:9-10). These martyrs are reigning with Christ in heaven, not for one thousand literal years but *completely, totally*.

The RSV has translated verses 4-5 in a very misleading way. It reads "come to life." The KJV, however, reads "lived"; this is closer to the original Greek and fits the context much better. These martyrs do not "come to life" but rather they "live" and experience a special reward others do not enjoy (cf. v. 5). This state is described as the "first resurrection," which seems to indicate a special reward for those who committed themselves to God and Christ completely. This reference to a "first" resurrection is not to be understood chronologically, but rather it indicates a special state of being or existence. The "second death" holds no terror for these people.

This "second death" clearly refers to a death other than physical death, which is the death that all humans must experience. Those who give their lives for the cause of God do not fear the second death, which is spiritual death, separation from God forever, suffered by those who make the wrong choice in the great cosmic struggle. Those who make the right choice and who remain faithful reign with Christ for "a thousand years" (v. 6).

20:7-10: If the interpreter understands this segment of the text as part of a chronological scheme, the translation "When the thousand years are ended" is quite acceptable and preferable. The problem, however, stems from the fact that the Greek text does not have an indicative verb here and therefore should *not* be translated in this way. The verb is subjunctive, indicating doubt or contingency, and a more precise translation is something like, "Whenever the thousand years may (would, could, should) end." The ending of the thousand years is contingent upon something. In this passage and in the book of Revelation as a whole, the complete dedication of God's people to God and against Satan and his cohorts is the means whereby Satan is bound and ultimately defeated. In Revelation also is the continuing plea for God's people to remain faithful and *not* become apostate. In this passage apostasy leads to the loosing of Satan and further persecution of God's people. When apostasy arises, Satan is loosed to pursue his wicked ways. Evil exercises its hideous power through willing human agents.

In short, this passage (and that in 20:1-3) is not part of a chronological scheme but rather is composed of episodes, which teach the reader or hearer something about the importance of faithfulness and loyalty to God and Christ and the consequences of falling away from that commitment. The author has been describing such a time when demonic evil appears to have the upper hand and when the complete loyalty of everyone associated with God's people is needed to keep the evil from becoming worse.

A related problem is the identification of "Gog and Magog." What or who are these mysterious entities?

Are they predictions of nations or people to come in the future? Or are they again descriptive of the persecutor? Why are these figures used? If one recalls that the term "Gog and Magog" comes from Ezekiel (chs. 38–39) and that the term there describes the persecutor of the Hebrew community at that time and that the persecutor of God's people in Ezekiel's time was Babylon, it is not difficult to ascertain why John chose this term here. In the setting of John's time, there was (as he has already made clear at several points) a new Babylon, a new persecutor of God's people. For John to use the figure of Gog and Magog here is not surprising and certainly not to be understood as a prediction of some entities to come in the future. John is still talking about his present persecutor, Rome.

Also in this section there is another reference to gathering for battle. The evil persecutors surround the "beloved city," but no battle is ever fought. As in 16:14-20, there is a gathering but no battle. Here fire comes down from heaven and consumes the evil besiegers of God's people. (It is interesting to note also that there is no mention here of Armageddon.) There is a sense of finality, however, in that the persecutors are removed and given their reward—a permanent place in the lake of fire and brimstone to dwell forever with those with whom they have cast their lot and dedicated their ultimate commitment. The idea is one typical of justice as understood in the biblical writers. The penalty fits the crime, and those who sin are turned over to that sin! Those who choose evil are allowed and required to remain with their choice.

20:11-15: To this point in chapter 20, the reader has found none of the components of the Darbyist interpretation of this passage. There is no return of Jesus, no absolute binding of Satan (and none by Jesus), no thousand-year *earthly* reign, no final battle that ends all human history. The only way one can find those ideas in this text is to import them—and that is not an option for anyone who is attempting to understand what the text originally said and meant.

The interpreter may be by this time so skeptical of the Darbyist scenario that any thought of a final judgment could be put aside. It is interesting, however, that this last segment of the passage does in fact depict a final judgment. The text does not indicate whether this judgment takes place in one huge scene at one particular time or whether the passage simply teaches that all people at one time or another must face the judgment of God. But face God's judgment they must. When they do, they will be required to answer one basic question: Did you ally yourself with God and God's purposes, and did you remain faithful to God, especially in times of persecution? This is what is meant by the verse, "And the dead were judged by what was written in the books, *by what they had done*" (v. 12*b*, emphasis mine). There is no thought here of a "work's righteousness" as some have attempted to find. The context of Revelation (and the entire body of the Scriptures) rules out that idea. To remain faithful in the midst of adversity is the single criterion (in this book) used to determine one's standing in God's judgment.

The "second death" is explained now as the "lake of fire." It is that place where the powers and forces of evil reside along with those who have allied themselves with those forces. The place is described symbolically as a "lake of fire" since fire in Jewish literature frequently represented the judgment of God or the means for the disposition of those who opposed God, or both. In short it is a place, or perhaps better a state of existence, apart from God, a place people have made a conscious choice to enter by their negative response to God and their refusal to dissociate themselves from evil.

21:1-4: After the description in chapter 20 of the removal and judgment of the persecutor, John now turns to describe the new age the Christians will experience and what will be expected of them in it. The new age is made possible because a "new" or "transformed" "heaven and earth" have been created by the removal of the sea. The strange reference here to the "sea being no more" is John's way of saying apocalyptically that the persecution was over. After all, where had the persecutor (the beast) originated? From the sea (cf. ch. 13)!

The new age is to be characterized by God's presence with the people and the persecution gone. This new age is symbolically depicted in a description of the new Jerusalem coming down from heaven to earth. What John is about to describe is an earthly scene, not a detailed atlas of heavenly places. (One notes the way modern interpreters have reversed these descriptions.) It is a portrait of a new age described in typical apocalyptic symbolism whereby the people of God can go about their duties and responsibilities without fear of persecution by the forces of evil.

This new age is characterized by a renewed sense of the presence of God. The tears and pain of persecution are over. The idea of this scene that "death will be no more" is not to be understood as a description of heaven. Rather the death that is alluded to here is not physical death in the "normal" and natural sense, but it is a reference to the martyr's death—the basic kind of death that has been discussed in Revelation up to this point. The threat of martyrdom is now passed. The new age has dawned.

21:5-8: In this section the reader finds a reiteration

of several motifs from other parts of the book, which basically point toward the greatness of God and the surety of protection for those allied with God. There is another warning for those who ally themselves with evil. It is interesting that the list of human beings and their evils begins with "the cowardly," particularly appropriate for those to whom John is writing in a period of persecution. As for the Greek word translated in the RSV as "polluted," this may be a reference to emperor worship. There is the added reminder that those allied with evil will suffer the second death in the lake of fire. This second death represents a final and definitive separation from God.

21:9-14: Here John begins his detailed description of the new Jerusalem, which again descends from heaven to earth. If one is committed to literalism and chronological detail in interpreting this book, a problem is encountered here in that two Jerusalems are seen coming down to earth. In apocalyptic, however, the interpreter should not worry about such matters since apocalyptic scenes are often repetitive.

The city itself is described as structured around the number 12. There are twelve gates, twelve angels, names of twelve tribes and twelve apostles, and so on. It is evident that this city is special for the people of God, and the figures are basically taken from the books of Isaiah and Ezekiel (cf. Isaiah 60 and Ezekiel 48), where the new age is described as centering in a "new" Jerusalem.

21:15-21: The measuring rod is again used as a symbol of protection for those within the measured area. The interesting aspect of this is that the city is not only based on the number twelve, but it is described as a cube. In the Scripture there is another place that is a cube—the Holy of Holies, that place shrouded in mystery where the Presence of God dwells at all times but which could be entered only once a year and that by the priest to make atonement for the sins of the people. This city is the city where the Presence of God continuously dwells with all the people whom God has redeemed and who have been faithful and loyal.

In verses 19-20, the foundations are described as adorned with precious stones. The exact meaning of these stones is highly debated. Are they representative of the twelve stones in the breastplate of the high priest of Judaism? Are they representative of the signs of the zodiac? Is there any special meaning in the order in which they are listed? Some have argued that these stones did represent at that time the twelve stages of the zodiac, but the peculiar fact is that they are here listed in exactly the reverse order from the usual sequence. Scholars differ in their assessment of a special meaning for this figure. It does add some drama and significance to the image, but the association with the number twelve as special for God's people is the most important idea even if others may be understood.

It is clear where the figure of the huge pearls, which serve as the gates of the city, originates. The rabbis believed that pearls of enormous size would be found in the gates of the new Jerusalem. The picture of the streets of gold, "transparent as glass," is well known. Again the imagination and brilliance of the author can be seen in describing gold as clear.

21:22-27: This component of the passage emphasizes two ideas. First, there is the emphasis that in this new Jerusalem there is no Temple. A temple is a finite object limited by time, space, and geography. One has to go to that place to worship and to experience the presence of God. In the new age with the persecution gone, God's Presence will be available to all people wherever they are. One does not go to a place to worship; everything that one does should be understood as an act of worship. Worship too is a "state of being" rather than a chronological act.

A new situation has been created to allow the second point of emphasis to be realized, namely the bringing to the nations the light of God and the Lamb. These dwellers in this new Jerusalem invite all to come in, but those who continue to practice "abomination and falsehood" are not allowed to be a part of this new community; not because they are unwelcome but because they have excluded themselves through their choice of allying with evil.

The references in this passage to "nations" and people who practice and pursue evil cause some interpreters much difficulty. If one believes that the world has come to an end in chapter 20 with the "great battle," this situation causes a problem. There are those who actually rearrange the text in such a way as to present a logical chronology so that this problem is "solved." If the interpreter understands the basic nature of apocalyptic, however, there is really no problem here to explain.

22:1-5: The last component of this apocalyptic unit clearly emphasizes that the persecution, now having been removed, is no longer an obstacle for the people of God in the execution of their duty. That duty is to take God's revelation to the world, to offer new life to all nations. That is the responsibility always of God's people. At certain times the difficulties in fulfilling that duty make the task extremely hard; at other times the task is not so hard. The only thing needed is for the people of God to do what they have been called to do. After all, the leaves of the tree are "for the healing of the nations," and there are twelve kinds of fruit; that is, this scene depicts the work of God's people to call others to be a part of God's community. The conclusion looks forward once again to the ultimate victory already won by the Lamb but which will be shared with those who remain loyal to the Lamb and God's cause.

Part X: Epistolary Epilogue (22:6-21)

John concludes his apocalypse, which he has set within the medium of a letter (cf. 1:4-11), with this epistolary ending. It contains urgent appeals for those to whom this writing is addressed to remain faithful—to not become apostate—for the time for the removal of the persecutor is near. Interestingly enough the words *near* and *soon* appear five times in this short passage, and descriptions of what the faithful must do or not do also emphasize the nearness motif.

22:6-9: The author testifies in characteristic apocalyptic fashion on the heavenly origin of these visionary scenes. The emphasis here is on the nearness of these events. Actually it is only one event that the author has in mind—the removal of the persecutor so that these people who have suffered for the faith may be relieved of this pressure.

There is again the scene where John falls down to worship the angel and is told not to do that. Only God is to be worshiped.

22:10-17: Most apocalyptic works are pseudonymously written, usually in the name of some ancient worthy so that the visions in those books are to be "sealed up" until the appropriate time (cf. Dan. 8:19, 26). Since Revelation is not pseudonymous the order not to seal up the words is another means by which the author emphasizes the nearness of what he has described. The time is so short, indeed, that there is really little time left for any changes to be made (cf. vv. 10-11).

The idea of God's judgment is very clear in verses 12-15. All people will have to give account concerning which side they chose in the great cosmic struggle and bear the consequences of whatever choice was made.

John offers once again the call of Jesus for all to "come." There are no limitations on who can participate; the invitation is "free." Unfortunately not everyone will accept God's gracious offer extended through the Christ.

22:18-21: Verses 18-19 contain a typical apocalyptic warning about "adding to" or "taking away" from the words of the book. This is done to assure those for whom the book is written that the persecution will soon come to its end. These words are not a curse to be used by those who wish to frighten anyone who disagrees with their particular interpretation of Revelation. It is unfortunate that many have used them in such a misguided manner.

The book concludes with the promise, "I am coming soon," and a blessing on the saints. This raises once again the question of whether the author of Revelation believed that he was describing the final return of Jesus. Through the years, perhaps most interpreters of Revelation have understood John to be teaching just that. If so, then John was wrong. A careful reading of the book cannot lead to any conclusion except that John believed that what he was describing (however one interprets these visions) was to come *soon.* No amount of redefining "soon" and "near" can change that clear teaching. Therefore if John believed that the final return of

Jesus was to take place soon, he was mistaken. The argument that John believed that but God's revelation to him was really for the distant future is also invalid. On that interpretation, violence can be done to any text in the entire Bible to bend it to mean whatever the modern interpreter wants it to mean. No, if John really believed that what he had described was the final return of Jesus, he was wrong. History and the facts of history are clearly against him. And it is possible to interpret Revelation in this way. If one does that, however, what value does such a book have for us today? The obvious answer to that question is—none!

There is another way of understanding this teaching, however. If one consistently applies apocalyptic interpretative procedure to these visions and teachings, the very real possibility is that John did not understand himself to be describing Jesus' *final* return. He may have been using the apocalyptic idea of God or God's agent (in this case, clearly Jesus) in a symbolic way to describe the end of a period of persecution and the establishment of a new age with the persecution gone. If this is the case, then John is absolutely correct. According to most scholars and the teaching of the early church fathers, John wrote this book about A.D. 94–95. The emperor Domitian died in A.D. 96 and with his death the persecution ended. John had insisted all along that the end of the ordeal was near but that it still had a short while to run (cf. 6:11; 17:10). If this is John's intent, he is absolutely correct in his assessment of the situation. It is also clear that his use of apocalyptic ideology and symbols is consistent with what he has been trying to say to the people to whom he is writing.

John's basic appeal to the people was for them to

remain faithful to God and Christ, to continue to witness properly even in the midst of those harsh times. His promise to these people was not that they each would escape all danger or injury, but rather that the community would survive and be strengthened because of individual sacrifice. John assures those who had paid or would pay the supreme sacrifice that there is a special reward for each one—described by numerous apocalyptic images—to be in the presence of this great and majestic God forever (under the altar in heaven) and to reign with Christ for a thousand years.

The essence of any apocalyptic work, then, is that the ultimate victory belongs to God and that those who commit themselves to God will share in the fruits of that victory.

CONCLUSION

Because of the prevalence of the system of interpretation known as Darbyism (or dispensationalism) and
because that system and elements of that system
became a part of other systems (notably of many of the
adventist sects and of those who call themselves
fundamentalists) many persons are confused and even
troubled by what they know about the book of
Revelation. Some have reacted so negatively against
what has been popularly espoused that they have
ignored or even rejected Revelation altogether. Others
who have "bought into" the popular understandings
are puzzled, troubled, and even outraged to learn that
that system is relatively new and that it is, in most
aspects of the interpretation of Revelation, wrong.

The strong belief of some is that they do not believe
that the Darbyist system is wrong, while others feel
cheated not to have learned about an apocalyptic
interpretation until lately. The most asked question
usually is, Why hasn't someone told us this before?
Answers to that honest question are not simple. One
of the problems lies in the fact that many apocalyptic
works were not really discovered and studied until
the late nineteenth and early twentieth centuries.
Examination of these noncanonical works helped
immensely in learning about the basic nature and
method of apocalyptic writing. Understanding how
to interpret apocalyptic properly is in reality a fairly

recent development. It is only in recent years that main-line seminaries have added courses on apocalyptic to their curricular offerings. Further, even when pastors did understand Revelation and Daniel and other parts of the Bible correctly, they did not dare in some areas to "rock the boat" for fear of stirring up unwanted trouble. The best course of action seemed to them to be to "let sleeping dogs lie." Although their motives may have been acceptable, their silence has allowed the fanciful and misleading interpretations of Revelation to continue and to spread. Dedicated and sincere as the advocates of such interpretations of Revelation and other parts of the Bible are, they are wrong to impose into the text meanings that are not there and were never intended by the inspired writer. And it is wrong now with all that is known about apocalyptic to allow such misuses of the book to continue without challenge.

The message of apocalyptic is one of hope based on a magnificent vision of the greatness and power of God, who is just, righteous, good, merciful, and who rules over the created order even if it sometimes appears to the contrary. The book of Revelation is no exception to that pattern. The book is a classic example of this type of literature, and it was meant to give hope and courage, along with challenge, to the people for whom it was originally intended. The book is still relevant for today since the principles and teachings of the book are true anywhere persons are persecuted for their witness for God and Christ and their stance against evil and its forces.

There are many people who are extremely disappointed to learn that Revelation does not contain a blueprint for the end of the world, the return of Jesus, and all those other concepts that have become so closely identified with the "end-times." Many express the reaction "Is that all?" when learning what the book actually says. What John taught us in Revelation may not be so dramatic as some have led us to believe, but what he taught is much more realistic and in line with other biblical teachings. It is, after all, not insignificant to learn that God is in control of all creation, that God will win the final victory over evil, that those who are faithful will not have died in vain, that their witness is indeed part of God's victory.

Perhaps the reason why many people today do not feel the importance of the message of Revelation, which is basically directed toward people under persecution, is that very few people in our society are in fact persecuted. Harassed, bothered, annoyed, the object of sometimes cruel jokes, yes; but persecuted to the point of losing their lives, no. Among those who have experienced the horror of real persecution, however, the great message of Revelation can be appreciated with deep feeling. They would not say at the end of a period of intense persecution, "Is that all?" They would feel that a new age had dawned, that the horrors of the evil they had experienced were gone and none too soon. One can think of numerous examples from our modern "sophisticated" world— the Holocaust, the Gulags, cruel torturers such as the Amins, Khomeinis, and their kin. People who have been rescued from these horrors know what it means to experience a "new age" where persecution is gone.

There are other people who find apocalyptic thought and writing repulsive. To be sure, there is an element of "vengeance" to be found in these works. The cry from the persecuted, both the living and those already martyred, is "How long?" before God brings the evil people to judgment. This is not a request on the part of the persecuted to execute the judgment themselves, however. Rather it is a cry for God's justice to become effective in the world. It is a cry of righteous indignation of which there are numerous examples in other biblical books (cf. Nahum, the laws of the Torah, and even the teaching of Jesus, e.g., Matthew 23). Apocalyptic is really no more vindictive than any of the other biblical teachings; in apocalyptic times, however, the issue is more pressing and intense.

In the final analysis Revelation reflects the basic apocalyptic thought-pattern. There is a cosmic struggle between good and evil constantly in progress. All are compelled to ally themselves with one side or the other—and apocalyptic tells the story from the side of God and those who have chosen to ally themselves with God. The great seer of Revelation has caught a glimpse of the majesty and power of this God so that he truly believes that the ultimate victory belongs to God. Those who remain faithful and loyal will share in that victory. The evil are given the opportunity to repent; this delays the elimination of the persecution, so the faithful are urged to remain loyal, not to become apostate. If one renounces the faith and goes over to the other side, serious consequences will ensue. For those who remain faithful, even to death, there is a special reward. They will participate in the thousand-year reign with Christ, which is a state of being with God and Christ, a relationship that transcends physical death and in fact conquers it.

For those who renounce God there are serious consequences to be suffered. To cut oneself off from God, the source of life and all that is "good," carries with it the penalty of having to remain with the powers and forces of evil in the "place" (or perhaps better, a state of existence) set aside for them. In

Conclusion

Revelation this is called the "lake of fire." The book of Revelation reminds us that these are ultimate decisions people must make, and with ultimate consequences.

John primarily emphasizes in Revelation the greatness and majesty of Almighty God and the joy that can be experienced by those who ally themselves with God and the Lamb. In spite of all the hideous and horrible evil in the world, this God reigns supreme over all, and the ultimate victory over evil has already been won through the work of God in Christ. On a smaller scale, those who are faithful also are part of this victory. In the struggle there may be moments when the faithful are called on to make the great sacrifice, humanly speaking, on behalf of God and Christ, but the "first death" holds no terror for God's people. They shall be with God and Christ always. As John tells his readers and hearers in the middle of his book, "The kingdom of the world has become the kingdom of our Lord and of his Christ, and he shall reign for ever and ever." Hallelujah, Amen!

An Approach to Studying Revelation

If one really wishes to promote excitement and draw a larger than usual crowd for Bible study, the certain answer for success is to announce a study of the book of Revelation. Church members, when asked by leaders what they want to study, perhaps most frequently answer "Revelation(s)." Many of these people are genuinely concerned about understanding the book properly and realize that the exotic symbolism and imagery, coupled with the popular and pervasive (mis)interpretations, have them completely confused and frustrated. Others want the study so as to reinforce their preconceptions and already formed conclusions or to "set the teacher straight" on the "proper" understanding of the book. If a teacher expects to make everyone happy in examining the book of Revelation, that idea should be placed aside as an unattainable dream. If, however, a teacher wishes to examine the book of Revelation carefully and honestly, and is willing to accept the problems that will arise, the experience can be extremely rewarding both for the teacher and for most of the participants in the study.

There is no magic formula that can miraculously solve all the problems attendant to a study of Revelation, but the following outline and guidelines have been used with some success by leaders who have risked the dangers of such an endeavor.

First of all, and perhaps most important, the leader

133

must have studied diligently and must have come to a "comfortable" understanding of Revelation before attempting to teach it to others. To this end there are numerous commentaries that can and should be consulted. Not all books on Revelation are responsibly written, and some should not be consulted except to illustrate how the "popular" viewpoint uses (or rather misuses) the book. (To assist in this study, a bibliography of good commentaries and other books is supplied following the conclusion of this chapter.) It must be noted here and emphasized that no two commentators will fully agree on all the details of a book so filled with symbols and images. In the text of this book, for example, no attempt was made to interpret every symbol, partly because it is difficult in apocalyptic to identify with preciseness those symbols that really stood for some specific idea or person or event, and so forth, and those symbols that were used simply to enhance the overall drama of the scene. Such is the nature of apocalyptic literature. If the main emphases are understood correctly, however, debates over smaller matters can be handled without major problems.

Another highly effective component in a successful study of Revelation is to present a brief history of the current popular views and where they originated, how they developed, what their presuppositions are, and so on. Several books can be helpful in this regard and these are specified here: Dewey Beegle, *Prophecy and Prediction;* Ernest Sandeen, *The Roots of Fundamentalism: British and American Millenarianism, 1800–1930* (which is unfortunately out of print presently); and James M. Efird, *End-Times: Rapture, Antichrist, Millennium.* From the Darbyist perspective, C. C. Ryrie, *Dispensationalism Today,* is a very readable and honest book. Understanding that approach is crucial since so much of the popular thinking today about Revelation traces its roots to Darbyism.

The study itself should be carefully structured, primarily centering on the self-contained visionary units in the book. Once the apocalyptic thought-pattern is grasped and the major symbols explained, the group is ready to look at the text itself. There is no substitute for examining the text carefully since so many of the popular ideas about Revelation are not based on the text but on preconceived ideas of what the text says. The best defense against those who want to impose a foreign system and ideology on any text is to use the text as the basis for the study. For example, there are those who want to find in Revelation a final battle that ends all history. If one examines the text carefully, one finds that no such battle is described and that history continues. If someone wishes to believe that there will be a great battle to end all history, that is fine. But do *not* read that into the text of Revelation; that idea is not there. It is unfair to any text to read into it ideas that were never intended. That is especially true of the biblical writings.

In conducting a study of Revelation, the approach to take is simple. Learn as much as possible about the book and how it has been interpreted. Be careful to lay a solid foundation for apocalyptic ideology and literary method. Divide the book into manageable units (as John did) and study each one in the light of how the original author, readers, and hearers would have understood that message in their own time and place. Finally, insist on a consistent apocalyptic interpretation of the book; that is, understand the writing as a symbolic work presented in a specific literary style and thought-pattern, which must be interpreted throughout in the light of that style.

Such a study will be rewarding and exciting for the participants. It will not, however, be without controversy. The Darbyist system of interpretation is widely known and has been accepted by many persons, most of whom do not know its origins or its presuppositions. These people have based their "faith-security" system on this type of understanding of Revelation (and other passages that have been added from other parts of the Bible). Any questioning of their understanding is not a matter for objective discussion but is a threat to their entire faith system. Because of this the response of these people is usually rather belligerent to say the least.

If this system of interpretation is allowed to continue unchecked and unchallenged, however, simply to avoid controversy, the book of Revelation (and other parts of the Bible as well) will be left to those who, though very sincere, misinterpret these texts very badly. Good positive study of apocalyptic literature such as Revelation, Daniel 7–12, and other passages will lead to better understanding of this material and will deepen one's faith—a trust relationship between the believer and God that cannot be broken by the worst that the powers of evil can do. It must be made clear to all that this *relationship* is the key to "security," not a fantastic interpretation of the marvelous book of Revelation. If the study accomplishes only that, it will be well worth the effort.

BIBLIOGRAPHY

Commentaries

Beasley-Murray, G. R. *The Book of Revelation.* New Century Bible Commentary Series. Grand Rapids: Wm. B. Eerdman's Publishing Co., 1981.

Beckwith, Isbon T. *The Apocalypse of John.* Grand Rapids: Baker Book House, 1967 (orig. ed. 1919 by Macmillan).

Caird, G. B. *A Commentary on the Revelation of St. John the Divine.* New York: Harper & Row, 1966.

Charles, R. H. *The Revelation of St. John.* 2 vols. International Critical Commentary. Edinburgh: T. &. T. Clark, 1920.

Collins, A.Y. *Crisis and Catharsis: The Power of the Apocalypse.* Philadelphia: Westminster Press, 1984.

Fiorenza, Elisabeth S. *Invitation to the Book of Revelation.* Garden City, N.Y.: Doubleday, 1981.

Ford, J. M. *Revelation.* Anchor Bible Series. Garden City, N.Y.: Doubleday, 1975.

Kiddle, Martin. *The Revelation of John.* Moffatt New Testament Commentary. Naperville, Ill.: Alec R. Allenson, 1940.

Mounce, Robert. *The Book of Revelation.* New International Commentary Series. Grand Rapids: Wm. B. Eerdmans Publishing Co., 1977.

Sweet, J. P. M. *Revelation.* Philadelphia: Westminster Press, 1979.

Books on Apocalyptic and Its Interpretation

Collins, John Joseph. *The Apocalyptic Imagination: An Introduction to the Jewish Matrix of Christianity.* New York: Crossroad Books, 1984.

Hanson, Paul D. *Old Testament Apocalyptic.* Interpreting Biblical Texts Series. Nashville: Abingdon Press, 1987.

Rowland, Christopher. *The Open Heaven: A Study of Apocalyptic in Judaism and Early Christianity.* New York: Crossroad Pub. Co., 1982.

Rowley, H. H. *The Relevance of Apocalyptic.* 3rd ed. New York: Association Press, 1964.

Russell, D. S. *The Method and Message of Jewish Apocalyptic.* The Old Testament Library. Philadelphia: Westminster Press, 1964.

Schmithals, Walter. *The Apocalyptic Movement: Introduction and Interpretation.* Trans. John E. Steely. Nashville: Abingdon Press, 1975. (Unfortunately this book is out of print but is especially useful if available.)

Books on Darbyism and the Darbyist System

Bass, Clarence B. *Backgrounds to Dispensationalism: Its Historical Genesis and Ecclesiastical Implications.* Grand Rapids: Wm. B. Eerdmans Publishing Co., 1960.

Beegle, Dewey M. *Prophecy and Prediction.* Ann Arbor, Mich.: Pryor Pettengill, 1978.

Efird, James M. *End-Times: Rapture, Antichrist, Millennium.* Nashville: Abingdon Press, 1986.

Rowden, Harold H. *The Origins of the Brethren, 1825–1850.* London: Pickering & Inglis, 1967.

Bibliography

Sandeen, Ernest R. *The Roots of Fundamentalism: British and American Millenarianism, 1800–1930*. Chicago: University of Chicago Press, 1970.

Books from the Darbyist Perspective

Lindsey, Hal. *The Rapture: Truth or Consequences*. New York: Bantam Books, 1983.
———. *There's a New World Coming*. Santa Ana, Cal.: Vision House Publishers, 1973.
Lindsey, Hal, with C. C. Carlson. *The Late, Great Planet Earth*. Grand Rapids: Zondervan Publishing House, 1971.
Ryrie, C. C. *Dispensationalism Today*. Chicago: Moody Press, 1965.
Walvoord, John F. *The Blessed Hope and the Tribulation*. Grand Rapids: Zondervan Publishing House, 1976.
———. *The Revelation of Jesus Christ*. Chicago: Moody Press, 1966.

LaVergne, TN USA
10 February 2010
172686LV00002B/11/P